Forward

These are some of the genteel phrases

- "Geeez-oh... John Muir hud his heid   ....,

- "This bike was built for Giants – you have to get it Telt!"..... and of course

- **"That's how we do it in Vegas Baby!"**

Is it a travel book? Yes, it is a travel book in as far as it describes a Harley Davidson Trip covering a thousand miles of Western USA. However, it also not a travel book but a narrative of the trip of a lifetime for a normal Scotsman, running from the lunacy of Las Vegas; through the majestic Desert; the mighty Yosemite; the old-style of San Francisco; the biker's dream of the Big Sur and the total and utter madness of L.A.

For potential bikers, each chapter has some facts about places to go, potential pitfalls and is perhaps a guide to anyone thinking of doing a similar trip. The fun part is a series of narratives (with more than a little Scotsman's skew) sent back to Scotland during the trip. Some of the ridiculous anecdotes will raise a smile whereas others will show the difficulties that a biker or tourist could find along the way. I hope that they also convey the sense of surprised, wonder that I felt far more often than I could have predicted, along the way.

Whether you are an experienced biker, someone contemplating a similar trip, or just looking to hear some heartfelt or amusing anecdotes, I hope you will enjoy this book. Of my travels so far, this one has been the most varied and fun.

Contents

7. Big Sur

A Biker's dream, a Hiker's dream, wonderfully scenic, wildlife abundant......
and Bloody Freezing!

8. San Luiz Obispo

How do they do that – is it a Film Set?

9. L.A. 1 - The Freeway

Don't do it man!

10. L.A. 2 – Santa Monica

Venice Beach – just a big version of the beach at Ayr, Scotland?..... or the
most wonderful mixture of Lunatics ever?

Preface – The Route and Planning Ahead

Before we get going on the story, a quick look at the route that I took and a few words of advice.

If you are contemplating a bike trip, you need to plan.... plan, plan, plan - with the first thing being your route. It is very important to know where you are going and research it prior to embarking. Going on a tour alone can be dangerous for one thing. But the main reason I think planning is essential is to make sure you don't *miss* anything. Touring around looking for sites to see, or worse, trying to find a hotel at the end of a hard day's ride can completely ruin your trip.

This book is not written to recommend the route that I took. If you are going on a trip you need to decide the route yourself. You may read on and decide you do want to do the same trip; incorporate some of it into your own trip; or ignore it completely. The main thing is that the choice has to be yours – it's your trip!

You may have noticed another book of similar content coming out recently, written by another Scotsman affectionately known as "The Big Yin".... of course I mean Billy Connolly not my mate Big RRRoddy.

Well he chose Route 66 which takes you clear across America from Chicago in the East, to Los Angeles in the West. This appeals to many and would be a great tour (if you can find it all.... pre-programmed Sat-Nav is a good idea). However, I chose the route shown below instead as it has such variety – Fiery Desert, Snowy Mountains, Major Cities, Winding Coastal Roads, Beautiful National Parks – the lot. Whatever route you choose, plan it well in advance. Give yourself the maximum chance of fitting in all the things you want to see and do and, above all – keep yourself safe.

One piece of advice I will give is **get a good book**. When I began planning this trip I bought only two things – a detailed map of Western

USA...... and *Lonely Planet California*. This book was £17 (about $34 dollars at the time) which I thought was a little steep. However, I had used Lonely Planet on several forays into darkest Eastern Europe following the magnificent but desperately unlucky Scotland Team (aye they are!) and I thought it might help.

The Lonely Planet book became my bible throughout the entire planning process and subsequently throughout the entire trip. At the planning stage, I could draw up a possible day's route using the map, then consult Lonely Planet to add the detail. It had information on every town, village and city on the route and also any local places of interest along the way. For a possible overnight stop I could find: not only accommodation ranging from tents to five star hotels; but also places worth visiting; where the shops were for supplies; any areas of town best avoided (let's face it – this is the U.S.) and, most importantly; where the best pubs are (let's face it - I'm Scottish). This made the planning of this trip far easier. *Lonely Planet* is written by real, travelling reporters who actually do the activities reviewed – dangerous or not - and stay in the flea-pits as well as the good hotels. The information is accompanied by a handy street map of each area so it is a useful companion to have *during* your trip too – you can't take your SatNav everywhere!
Well alright you can take your SatNav everywhere these days on your smart phone but you get the idea – being a stubborn old bugger, I won't rely solely on the bleedin' internet and like to use a street map and a compass now and again, even just to prove I can still do it!

In actual fact, I didn't even take a Sat-Nav with me on this trip at all as the map and *Lonely Planet* allowed me to plan it so carefully... and I'm actually still here!

 (I ought to be getting commission for this - *"Haw!.... Lonely Planet!.... Gonnae gei-us a wee dodd o' that commissiownnae!".*
For the English, Europeans, Americans and all other far better spoken races of this world, here is the first, and last, translation I will give in this book – *"Excuse me Lonely Planet Chaps, would you be so awfully*

kind as to consider my extensive promotion of your wonderful book and provide any monetary rewards as you see fit? There's good chaps.")

If you don't have the inclination or the time to fully plan your trip, I would recommend the next best thing – get a pre-planned tour with a Sat-Nav guide. Most of the bike hire outlets do this. At least then you will have somewhere to stay each night and a good idea of where the places of interest are. From what I've seen, most of these tours are pretty good. Guys working in Bike Hire Outlets tend to be Bike Enthusiasts and set out the tours to take you along routes suited to the Biker – not the Winebago-Wielders..... For a bit extra, they will actually ride with you which may suit the first timers.

If, however, you are the type who goes into everything gung-ho just to see what transpires – then good luck...... It might turn out to be the trip of a lifetime. Then again it might turn out to be a trip full of fuel shortages; mechanical failures; hotel searching; seeing nothing of interest; and getting ill from too much sun in the desert, too much snow in the mountains, or too much detergent in the cocaine you wake up and find all over you in the drug den you don't remember being taken to.....

Me? I don't like to waste any time (and consuming various Alcoholic Beverages in local Yee-Haw Establishments is not wasting time – it is called "sampling the rich cultural diversity of the locality"......) so for me, planning is key.

Obviously, a bit of thought needs to go into the gear you take with you too – especially if you are going through the desert then straight into the snowy mountains as I did. However, we will cover this later in the book.

For now - a look at the route, then on to the real stuff.....

Route Map

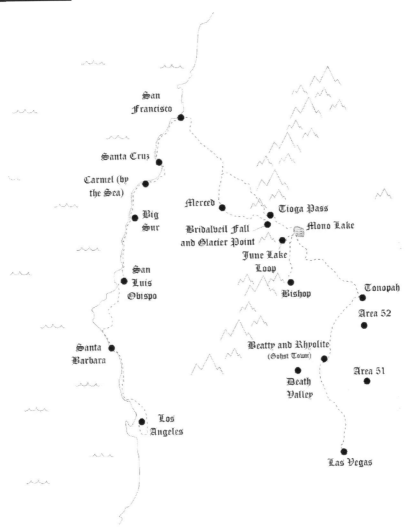

Note:

The Chapters in this book have two forms of writing. The sections in *italics* are tweets, emails and messages sent home in real-time throughout the trip - these range from informative comment down to downright idiocy..... The sections in between were written later to expand on what was happening at the time and to impart useful or interesting information to the reader. The tweets are aplenty in Chapter 1 as Vegas threw its madness at me. For the "Petrol-Heids", the bike tour story starts in Chapter 2….

Chapter 1 - The Pre-Ride Warm up............

VEGAS!!!!

"In terminal 5 at Heathrow. Having a cider. Big Rodders has long hair noo and looks like the lion from wizard of Oz...."

This was the humble beginning of the trip of a lifetime. I was meeting a very good friend at Heathrow whom I hadn't seen in a long while.

There was actually a group of 7 of us heading for Vegas for another very good friend's 40th Birthday. This was going to be fun and the "craic" was already good; but what I was really looking forward to was starting off on my solo bike trip four days later. I was due to pick up a Harley Davidson Electraglide on the Tuesday and was secretly as excited as Charlie Bucket heading for The Big Hoose! In the meantime there was Vegas to hit and, having not been there before I wasn't expecting too much – *Jeezo, Wiz Ahh Wroang.....*

But First, some History.

Las Vegas sits within the Las Vegas Valley – so called because of the presence of Artesian Wells (where deep ground water is pushed upwards towards the surface) which support areas of Green Meadow. In fact "meadows" in Spanish is "Vegas" – hence the name.

Contrary to what several Hollywood films would have you believe, Las Vegas, the town, was around long before the gambling and debauchery that has made it famous. There were several periods of organised habitation in the Las Vegas Valley throughout the later 1800s with Science Expeditions, Mormon Missionary Colonies and of course the ever-present US Army hovering around.
However, Las Vegas first became a proper Railroad Town in 1905 when the San Pedro, Los Angeles and Salt Lake Railroad Company

auctioned off some land for private use. This piece of land went on to become the downtown area of Las Vegas we know so well today.

Las Vegas was incorporated as a self-governing City in 1911 – long before the likes of Benjamin Seigel (Bugsy) began building Casinos. For a time it was the hub of mining activity in the area and a thriving railroad town but its importance waned as the railroad branched farther out. Later on though, with the influx of workers on the Hoover Dam arriving from 1931, coupled with the legalisation of gambling that same year, Las Vegas began to form into the place we know today.

The Hoover Dam was completed in 1935 – 2 years early which was quite a feat considering it was built during the Great Depression. This brought fresh tourism into Las Vegas.

There are suggestions that Las Vegas expanded rapidly in the 1940's due to the Manhattan Project. However, it is difficult to see how, what with the main research Laboratory of Los Alamos being 668 miles away in New Mexico and Alamogordo (the site of the Trinity Nuclear Test) 712 miles away. The nearest hub was at Inyokern – 238 miles to the West - which manufactured non-nuclear bomb components.
I think it more likely that this information really applies to the **1950**'s and the Nevada Test Range near Beatty. Between 1951 and 1992 there were 928 Nuclear Tests (at least that is how many were *announced)* there. Above-ground tests were allowed up until 1962 and the mushroom clouds from these could be seen from Las Vegas - almost 100 miles away. During this time, people would come to Las Vegas especially for "Atomic Explosion Parties......."

Hmmm.....

Anyway, on with the story....

   "Finally Landed. 38 degrees but a breeze...... Awesome....."

So, we had made it. In all, about 14 hours of fidgety discomfort, dampened by alcohol, films and some racy conversation..... However, things were not as I expected.....

I have never been a fairground type – I like a bit of culture with my football and beer…. and as such I didn't expect to particularly enjoy Vegas. Well that was the first of many assumptions to be smashed on this trip. After 4 days and nights with a total of 12 hours sleep, I was in love with the place. How to sum it up? Mmmmmm, not easy – the only way I can do it is to mention a complete polar opposite – the mighty *Rome.*

I have always said that everyone should try to visit Rome at least once in their lives. When I was in Rome, I found I could walk around any corner, up any alleyway, almost through any doorway and see something incredible. Wonderful things were all around from a time when Italians were extraordinarily organised, driven and clever (in contrast to the lackadaisical, shambles you often find nowadays in Rome's public organisations…. 2 hours to buy a train ticket?.... Come-on).

I would now recommend that, along with Rome, everyone should try to see **Vegas** at one point in their lives too……. for much the same reasons. The connection is nicely summed up by the film *Gladiator* by Ridley Scott. When encountering the mighty Colosseum in Rome for the first time, the Numidian slave is awe struck. He manages to mutter the phrase "I….... I didn't know men could....... ***build*** such things."

Well, being a bit of a Numidian slave myself, that is sort of how I reacted when seeing Las Vegas for the first time. As I turned each corner and was greeted by yet another outrageous sight, the word "Audacity" just kept springing to my mind. It is not just the incredible buildings – it's the sheer audacity of; for example, thinking up the idea of building a huge hotel in the shape of a fairytale castle – and **then actually going through with building it….!** Being a Civil Engineer I understand how massive an undertaking it is to carry out a *normal* development – let alone building a giant, indoor version of **Venice** – complete with canals, city streets, a false Viennese sky and even a night time town square with a festival going on………… 24 hours a day!

Yes it's fair to say I was often thunderstruck walking around Vegas. However, rather than the Numidian's classically styled phrase – all I could muster up was:-

- "What- in-the-name-of………."

- "Jeees-oh….." and;

- "Hoots Mon. Ah Canna get mah heid roon this at awww!"

(ok I threw the last one in for the tourists but you get the idea…..)

Anyway, after a very long double flight to Las Vegas we hadn't slept for a while. However, if you think you will have a quick sleep when you get to Vegas – Fogeddabowdidd! I defy anyone to arrive (as I did) in a hotel taxi-rank with a hundred thousand bright, white, light bulbs shining down on you (even in the daytime),…….. and then to go for a sleep. We were spread out in various hotels and it took perhaps half an hour for everyone to be back out and *oan the bevvy*.

To start with, we wandered in and out of a few casinos – what else would one do…? I had read a short book about the basic casino games (of which I had never had the slightest interest before) on the plane over and was itching to try some craps. The evening began with…..

"Just had a cracking game of Craps. Won a bit, lost a bit, won Mick a fortune rolling nines. Great crack. 2am, no sleep for 27 hours"

Which led on to:-

"Still in the bar. 29 hours. Thinking about another game of craps! Hope all is well"

Which led on to:-

"Just in with a Subway. 4.15am. Don't think I'll get you on phone tomorrow as I'll be asleep. X"

"as I'll be asleep"…..... ha ha Aye Right! Sleep is not possible in Vegas. It's not that there is noise keeping you up – the hotels are super-well-built. It is more the fact that you fall asleep (or more likely pass out) thinking that will be it for 7 or 8 hours, then wake up a short while later thinking "What am I missing?!!!" After perhaps 4 hours of being out cold, I became aware of the beat coming from the pool which led on to the first tweet of the following day very shortly after.

"Morning! At the hotel pool. Rap music pounding out of huge sound system. Sun beating down, Top-Heavy Luvlies everywhere. Sorry Lorraine/Mum...."

Hhmmmmmm. And finally:-

"Just been playing pool volleyball with a load of American Lads. Their top shout was "SHOT dude! Now THAT's how we do it in Vegas baby!!" and it was bloody catching!"

A couple of points - firstly, this method of categorising the cultural significance of an area, by the level of upper body, over-endowment of the females within; somehow carried on throughout my trip. Again, sorry Lorraine and Mum…. and in fact to all women on the planet…..

(It is not all my fault though. I believe I stole that genteel phrase from the excellent Chris Moyles show in the mighty nineties – so it must be his fault! Que the lawsuit...).

Secondly, I tend to be a bit like Marina Sirtis in "Star Trek the Next Generation" – a bit of an "Empath". I unknowingly absorb the mannerisms and general feeling of the people around me and begin to transmit it back. By the end of the game I had claimed the Vegas-Volley-Ball phrase for my own and found myself using it (complete with the two fingered, Devil's horns salute) around the Craps table that night. Curious…..

The point of all this is that Vegas has a sort of electric buzz going on all the time. You can't help but feel it, it carries you along and somehow makes you forget all your cares and just have fun….. If you slow down, you think you are missing something and the motor just kicks back into life again.

However, people tend to see Vegas as the home of gambling so best to touch on that first.

"Later-on I hit the Casino……"

Many of you will be familiar with Casino games. I was a complete novice when I entered Las Vegas and was a complete novice when I left. However, it didn't stop me enjoying myself and no heavy losses were sustained. As I mentioned above, I read a short book about Casino Games on the way over. This, combined with my experience while there, brings me to make two points to the novice first-time Casino-Goer:-

1.   Pick the games that give good odds and longevity – not the high risk high return ones.

The main thing I took from the book I read was that there are games where you can win a lot of money quickly, and games that you can take your time at and enjoy. I watched a friend win 100 dollars at Blackjack in about 5 minutes, then watched another lose about the same at Roulette in the same time. To me these games are high stakes, fast moving but dangerous….. The odds are against you and at a minimum of $10 per bet, can see you well down very quickly. To any first timers out there, the game I would recommend is **Craps**.

Now Craps also has its fair share of do-or-die, big return bets available where the odds are quite severely against you. However, it also has small return bets which have far better odds of paying off. While placing these easy bets, you get more skilled and you can begin to add in slightly higher risk and higher return bets at the same time. You do not need to augment the amounts you bet either which gives you the chance to play slowly and enjoy it.

The main thing I found about playing Craps though, is that it is FUN. When I was playing blackjack, or poker I was sweating and nervous – I could be up one hand, gone the next. However, the 2nd evening in Vegas I stayed at my gaff while the boys went to the Old Town and I had a great time with the "new friends" that I met around the Craps table (sad?.... Who me?). But that is the thing about Craps – it is SOCIAL. You've all seen the movies where they are all gathered around the Craps table and the beautiful "Bond Girl" is rolling the dice for a stern and handsome Baron of Evil while all the other players are hooting and cheering..... That's how Craps is in Vegas.

After each round, the dice passes to the next player around the table and he/she becomes the "Shooter" rolling for everyone until that round is over. What number the Shooter rolls affects the different players in different ways (except for the roll of the dreaded 7 when the house takes all). The right combination of numbers can win a solitary player a lot of money; while some numbers tend to please everyone at the table. For this reason, the game is LOUD. I found myself quickly joining in with the hoots of "ShooodderrrrRRRR" before each "Shooter" rolled the dice. The genteel phrase that I had so carefully memorised at the pool earlier made several appearances too. Altogether now.......
"That's how we do it in VEGAS, BABY!!!!"

On a float of only 30 dollars I played for 2 hours at the same table, with the same people. Drink is brought for free when you are gaming which for a Scotsman is like Valhalla - "win money and drink for nothing? – goan yersel!!!". In fact I tweeted:-

"Down to casino. $30 up at b/jack; played craps for 2hrs - $100 up at peak. Down to 6 up at the end. Full night's fun, didn't pay for single drink. Cool!"

Yes I was $100 up but I was having so much fun that I just kept on playing. I left the table with my original stake; a bit of a "heid" on (Scottish for being a tad tipsy what?); and was content with losing my winnings as I had had such a good time…..However, maybe it was just a lucky night as the next tweet read…..

"Just stuck a dollar in a one-cent fruit machine (about 0.6 of a pence per shot) and won 42 dollars - first time I've played one. ….."

If you are interested in how to play Craps, then here are the rules as I understand them….. If not then flick past this section like a teenager flicks past a footnote…

Craps – The Basics

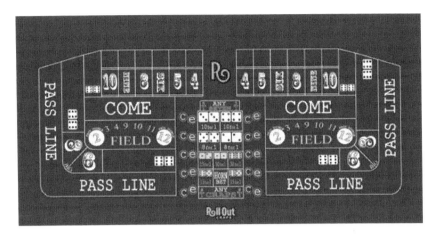

Without going into detail, you have to play the "Pass Line" bet to play. To do this you place a chip on the Pass Line. This will give you a 100% return if a 7 or 11 is rolled. You will lose your stake if "craps" is rolled (2, 3 or 12). If any other number is rolled then that becomes the "point" number and the game starts. They put a disc a bit like a Hockey Puck on that number at the top of the board to signify that it is the "point" number.

Once the game is in play, there are many different bets you can place. Everything continues until a 7 is rolled - this finishes the game and the dealer takes everything left on the table - or the point number is rolled.

 Aaah, the dreaded 7.... There are more combinations of two dice numbers that add up to 7, than any other number. If you don't believe me just try it - for 7 you can have 3 and 4; 5 and 2 or 6 and 1. Multiply this by two (for two dice) and you have six combinations. Then try it with say, 9. You can have 6 and 3, or 5 and 4. Multiply that by two dice and you have only four combinations. This means that 7 is more likely to be rolled than any other number. After 7 the next two likeliest are 6 and 8, then 5 and 9, and so on until you get to the least likeliest to be rolled - 12 and 2 which have only one combination each. Once the game is in play, the "Field Line" bet is a good one as the dice can come up with any of 3,4,9,10 or11 for you to get 100% return on whatever stake you put down. Even better, if a 2 or 12 is rolled, you get back **double** your stake. Hence you only lose your stake if a 5, 6, 7 or 8 is rolled. Herein lies the danger due to the likelihood of these numbers coming up. Despite this though, I won quite a lot playing the Field Line. To play this bet you just put your chips within the Field Line.

While toying with these bets you can also place a bet on a specific number. This bet can remain on the table until someone rolls the dreaded 7 (when all bets lose) or someone rolls the point number. Every time *your* number is rolled you win odds of 7:6. From my book I learnt that, due to the high number of possible dice combinations, you have the best chance of winning if you only place bets on 6 or 8. However, a friend of mine favoured 9 and I won him a load of money when I was the "Shooter" rolling nines over and over. To bet on a number you ask the dealer to put your chips on the number in question.

There are other higher risk, higher return bets too such as the "Hardways" or "One Roll" bets - these are the ones in the centre of the table - but I would tend to avoid these unless you are an expert or an adrenaline junkie. If you want to learn about Casino games for a visit to Vegas, I would certainly recommend the short book I read – "The Only Casino Games Worth Playing" by Ray Pesta.

End of Craps Rules – cease flicking…..

2. Do Summat Else!

This second point about gambling in Vegas is that you really don't have to do it at all. Yes, there are Casino tables everywhere you turn. But there are also incredible sights to see both outside and inside, and many activities to do. Apart from the amazing buildings and décor, there are piano bars (table top dancing bars), live bands, amazing dancing fountains, wonderful shows to visit, rides to go on…….

> *"We went on the rollercoaster on roof of New York New York earlier -*
> *a lot better/worse than expected. Maybe shouldn't have had a beer*
> *straight before….."*

This is an example of the sort of thing that you meet around every corner in Vegas: the rollercoaster actually built on the ROOF of the huge New York New York Hotel, Casino, Theatre and everything else Complex. You imagine this will be pretty tame as it is on top of a building (thereby giving it some novelty). Think again – it is pretty fast and had enough corkscrew action to impress my theme-park loving mate Rodders….. As another example of the madness of Vegas, if you look up from the rollercoaster you can see that on the side of a huge hotel, they have built a small Fairytale Castle, complete with Towers and Turrets. This just sits on the side of the hotel on its own.. I imagine it is there just in case a millionaire's daughter fancies being a fairytale Princess for the weekend and waking up in Repunzles tower of a morning…. Ahhh Vegas.

You can see the Spider-web of the Rollercoaster on the roof and in the background the fairytale castle on the side of the hotel.

It's hard to believe, but if you look a little further afield there are even several good museums based on Natural History, Indian Artefacts, Atomic Testing from the Manhattan Project era and so on. However, Vegas being Vegas, the one I saw the most fliers for was a little different. If you just aren't that into Historical Teachings but want to tell the folks back home that you have learned a little of the local historical culture – you could visit...... wait for it.......... The Mob Museum! In its own words it "presents an exciting and authentic view of the mob's impact on Las Vegas history and its unique imprint on the world.".... hmmmmm....... I think they should have one of these in Scotland – you could have "The Edinburgh Museum of the Slightly Unsavory Chaps that lived in those Ghastly Tunnels under the Royal Mile"

The point is (yes there is one), if you enjoy all of these things and the ones described further on, it results in reducing the time you spend gambling. If you are only gambling when you feel like it, rather than all the time, it is easier to give yourself a limit and stick to it.

Anyway, back to the Story........

The rest of the Vegas stay was just fun and entertainment. A few of the must-see (and perhaps must-avoid depending on your age and gender) sights are mentioned in the ever more bizarre tweets that followed as I got carried along by Vegas.

Bars

Las Vegas has a lot of bars and all seem to have some special quirk or other. After playing craps the 2nd night, I frequented a few which was an interesting little saga:-

> *" 2am. Just found a cracking piano bar. Full swing and dancing......Vegas....."*

Now this made a welcome change from the madness. A bit of musician-ship, twin baby-grand pianos and a lot of people singing along. I settled down. However........

> *"3.30am. Piano bar has changed into a classy, table-dancing, rap bar..... Aaaaah Vegas........."*

And then, later still

> *"Just dawned on me that the tables the Top-Heavy-Luvlies are dancing on are actually the two baby grand pianos from earlier. Can't go to bed now!."*

Yes at 3am, the piano lids were closed and the Piano's **themselves** became the podiums. The R and B and hip hop was cranked up and the Ugg boot clad, Top-heavy Luvlies magically appeared above the instruments. My reasoned argument that this instrumental, dual-furniture fact made it **impossible** to go to bed still seems quite plausible to me now.

There are Bars for everything in Las Vegas. One of my favourites was the Harley Davidson Bar where you are greeted from about half a mile away by the Giant front-end of a Harley Soft-Tail Classic which seems to have smashed through the wall above the door. When you get inside, it would take the most telly-deaf numpty not to notice the real, full-size Harleys that are hanging from a conveyor belt and float around the bar above your head, disappear into the ceiling then appear again lower down out of an opposite wall.

Nearby there is the Hard Rock Café with its 50 foot Gibson Les Paul pointing up into the sky; twinned with a 50-foot Coke Bottle next door.

There are countless Sports bars and gaming bars. I was quite surprised to see that many of the bars and Casinos seemed to have a constant supply of podium dancers above the tables – prompting the following reply tweeted from my wife:-

> *"Don't expect a table dancer when you get your dinner served up at home. Sounds like you're having a great time already - behave xx"*

Sexual Equality doesn't seem to apply to Vegas (so thanks for that) and the ladies seemed happy enough (I'm told pole dancing is a fabulous way to exercise though my wife doesn't agree). In all honesty, I didn't see the same stigma attached to these things in the States as there is in the UK - the women on the ground seemed quite happy that the girls were beautiful and doing a great job of showing it.

In fact, I found most people that I met in the US to be very happy to allow people to let their hair down, remembering ways that they used to do the same. In Vegas, the Desert, San Francisco, L.A.; they all seemed to have a "work hard play hard" attitude which wouldn't go amiss at times in the UK….

> *"7.30am Just heading home in burning hot morning sunshine amongst the joggers. Deffo overdone it this time. Scots vs American bar night!"*

This tweet (which I will explain in a minute) brings me nicely to my last point about the bars - everyone is there to enjoy themselves. I didn't see any trouble of any kind during my stay. Las Vegas seems to keep people's attention focussed on happy things all of the time. As a result, people seem to be able to drink a lot without the ugly side emerging.

Though I suspect that the Secret - I'm watching you – Casino-Police spirit offenders away like an owl swoops silently in for a vole; I can honestly say that I didn't even see a single episode of the disgruntled gambler throwing his weight around like Nicholas Cage in *Leaving Las Vegas*.

The above tweet was made after seeing-in the dawn with a prolonged drinking and arm-wrestling competition between my friends and the unlikely couple of an Avante-Garde Film Maker and his best friend the Iraq-bound soldier. Try doing that at 6am in a Glasgow bar lock-in…….. more likely to be a Jolly-Boy-John You-Tuber and a Northern Ireland veteran wi' the shakes…. "Whit? Arm Wrestlin'?... Try THIS!!!", zing!.... Aaaargghh….."

The only warning I would give is that Saturday night sees an influx of locals and gets a little heavier.

> *"Saturday night and everything is a bit harder. Brought the boys to a big open air bar that up to now has had a cracking band playing whenever I have passed it - 24 hours a day - but it's got a hard and heavy, underground, Techno DJ on now. Rotten. (And I LIKE Techno!)"*

However, we still didn't see any trouble – if you are there on a Saturday maybe that is the night to go to the show you have been thinking about, rather than hitting the bars…. unless of course you are a fan of hard and heavy, underground techno……

Themed Hotels

There are many incredible hotels in Vegas combining wonderful (if imitation) classic architecture and a host of things to do within. There are a few worth a mention before we move on to the bike tour.....

Stratosphere

At one point a friend took me out to the old town. This was the original Las Vegas downtown, before the development of the massive hotels and Casinos Southwards formed the Strip that is so well known today. Here, many of the Hotels look just that little bit jaded now. However, this is apparently where the serious gambling goes down – away from the madness....

There is still plenty to see though, such as the Circus Circus Hotel Complex, made famous by the James Bond film *Diamonds are Forever*. Here the Casino is actually within a giant Big-Top so don't be surprised when a trapeze artist skims over your head when you are about to roll a seven..... or were you...... "Tha' great swingin' nancy poot me aff!..." The oldest street in Las Vegas is the heart of the Downtown Area. Fremont Street is the scene that appeared in the title shots of almost every 70's and 80's film or cop show that had anything to do with Vegas. You can't help but recognise the huge, old signs made out of coloured bulbs such as the reclining cowgirl at Glitter Gulch or the Golden Nugget Casino sign. These days, around 5 blocks worth of Fremont Street is covered by the Viva Vision Canopy and Light Show. This is basically a massive, super-bright, curved screen that stretches for 5 Football Pitch lengths; has 12 million LED modules showing all manner of colours, patterns and films; and is accompanied by a 555,000 watt sound system. Not bad eh?

However, we were heading for ***The Stratosphere**. To put you in the picture, I knew that the Stratosphere was a huge tower that you could jump off on a wire – but that was it. You can get to within a block or two of it on the monorail which is clean, safe and cheap. I imagine that the walk from there to the Stratosphere or Circus Circus could be a little hairy at night but it was fine during the day when we went.

If you can imagine a 1000 foot high water tower – slender as it rises then top heavy like a golf tee with a marble on it – then that is the Stratosphere. There is a long spine protruding from the top which looks a little like a radio mast from the ground but I soon found out that it had a different purpose entirely.

"Been up the stratosphere - 1149 foot high tower. Going back the morra to jump off it on a steel rope....."

Two things to note: 1; say "the morra" in a Glasgow accent and the meaning will become clear and 2; if you come here and want to do the tower jump – book ahead.

"Can't do tower jump - too late."

See!

"Instead being fired up and down pole at very top then out over edge at high speed in wee car thing...."

So we went up the tower – this is impressive – really impressive. From the top you can look Southwards, right back to the Strip. You are way above all the towering hotels and (this is Vegas) they glint and sparkle in the sun, shouting their names at you. However, you also have a 360 degree view of the rest of Las Vegas. You can see how it has sprawled and spread out, and you realise – Las Vegas isn't just the strip – it is a City – full of the people who help everything to run as smoothly as it does. It is worth going up the tower ($16) for the view alone.

However,….. nothing prepared me for what was about to happen. The radio mast-like structure on the tip of the tower is a ride. You may have seen these in fairgrounds – basically there is a square ring of seats that sits around a big pole. This then carries people up the pole then drops them down a bit, then up a bit, then down and so on. I assumed that this would do the same – lift us up high and the view would be wonderful. ………. I was wrong.

We sat on the seats, they pulled a solid harness down over us, we looked bored, then……. Whoomp! I didn't expect the MASSIVE force propelling us upwards (as my ridiculously misshapen face belies on the photo the ride takes) but that wasn't the amazing part…
When you get to the top, you are weightless. The Super structure has been left far below, you can't see it, you can't see what's holding you in place, you can't see your feet – all you can see is Las Vegas from 1150 feet up, and you are *floating*. It feels exactly like you have been shot up into space…… The first thought that went through my head was "The machine has broken" – thinking we had broken free. My 2nd thought was that it was beautiful – like flying.
Only in Vegas would you find such a wild ride in such a crazy position – if your heart can stand it – try it. It's well worth the $13 ticket.

After that we tried the other ride. Basically, you sit in a car quite similar to a Rollercoaster car (just with some bits taken out of it so you can see straight down more easily… thanks for that). The car sits on a solid plane – which suddenly lifts up to form a slope of about 45 degrees – and you go shooting down it and off the edge of the tower. Now, as it starts to move, you know that it is going to stop at the end. By the time you are halfway down you are *hoping* it is going to stop at the end. By the time you get to the end you are convinced that it isn't going to stop and you are about to die…… I was especially worried as my friend Gandalf who was sitting next to me was at full rugby-weight and I feared for the shear-strength of the restraining bolts – again as the photograph belied….

Once you are out there though, you get to sit for a while. This was quite pleasant until my friend urged me to look over the edge of the car. Suddenly you realise that a few inches to your left or right is a 1000 foot drop…….

After that experience it was nice to find a large, circular bar in the heart of the round casino at the foot of the tower – nothing like a beer or four to calm the nerves. All in all the Stratosphere is definitely worth a visit – my advice – **go during the day.**

What is that thing on top? An antenna?...Aye Right!

Misshapen Faces at 4G and is it terror, or elation heading out over the edge in the Rollercoaster Car....... (I just know I shouldn't have put these pictures in).

The Venetian

How to describe the wonderful Venetian Complex? A mosaic-like maze of classic Italian architecture, colour and style? An indoor Italy sweeping you halfway across the globe to another time and a stylish pace? No, this classically Scottish tweet I sent sums it up better:-

"This place is mental. Indoor Venice complete with buildings, gondolas, false Italian sky. Can even go from day-time to night-time Venice through a door. Mental!"

In all honesty the Venetian *is* mental – pure radio-rental.
The outside of this complex is really quite pleasant. The whole building is made to look like a sort of Roman-esque Structure, but out in front there is a lovely river running below Venetian-style bridges and ivy clad walls. There is even pleasant, classical music drifting to your ears (which is quite a culture shock when you have just wandered out of Harrahs Casino next door in search of a bottle of water to cool the jets)....

When you walk in, the first thing you are confronted with is the Sistine Chapel...... ok it's not the Sistine Chapel and any Art Lovers among you would have a great pleasure in explaining that the art is more Michelob than Michelangelo. However, there is a beautiful domed ceiling painted in a wonderfully fresh mural that has you gazing up slack-jawed (or was that just me). You then find yourself in Venice..... There are canals, cobbled streets, balconies, a wonderful venetian sky with whispy clouds (this is the only thing that gives away that the ceiling is false – clouds? In Vegas???). The Gondoliers sing as they slowly punt their punters around.
In a state of overload-induced trance I wandered through the "streets" (we were indoors for crying out loud....), marvelling at the audacity of it all. Then bang; I went through a partition and found I had just lost 12 hours. I was now in a Venetian Town Square – a big one – and it was **night**...... There was a festival going on complete with Italian Choir,

town criers, and there were stars twinkling through the whispy clouds that you could just about make out in the night sky.

At this point in the afternoon I was reasonably sober (that is about as sober as it is possible to be in Vegas) and pretty keyed-up from the Stratosphere episode. However, I began to worry that I was losing it.......Erk!....... A swift exit back to daylight was required to bring reality back.

The Venetian is well worth a walk around – pretty impressive. What's amazing though is that this huge and wonderful place is only a small part of the hotel complex. In fact, at the time of writing this, the official Venetian Hotel website barely even mentions this place – it is only found under the heading of "Gondola Rides" and has only two small photos.... I can't imagine what delights await you in the 5 acre (yes I said 5 ACRE) pool area on deck 5 above......

The Venetian at Night and a few of the Bridges out front.

The first photo shows how realistic the sky is. The canals in the 2nd appear to go on for miles. The camera has picked out the shape of the ceiling in this photo but the eye couldn't.....

Shows

We all know that Las Vegas has big shows and huge sporting events. My advice though is to see a **Cirque de Soleil** show while you are there. These acrobatic extravaganzas of light, sound and human endeavour leave you utterly breathless.

To prove this point, the tweet I sent after seeing a show:-

"Shot straight up at 4G, 1000 ft up. Then Fired over edge of a tower on a rollercoaster car. Terrified. But that wasn't the most thrilling part of the day...
Cirque de Soleil. Look it up on net. Most incredible thing I have ever seen.

We couldn't get tickets for the show named "Ka" so went to "Zumanity" instead. This is a burlesque and was a bit naughty so be careful of you look it up. Aside from that though, I have never seen anything quite like it. It is hard to imagine that these things are even humanly possible, let alone actually dreaming them up to do in the first place.
To be honest it is barely describable - from the initial 2 nymph-like ladies, diving, swimming and doing acrobatics in what was basically a glass kitchen bowl about 2.5m across...; to the dwarf flying and spinning around your heads on strips of silk; to the robot man who actually rolled around the stage inside a metal hula hoop while doing acrobatics.... Big thanks to Rodders for introducing me to this!"

The Circue de Soliel show even surpassed the Stratosphere visit which I had done the same day. You sit there wondering how the human body can perform such acrobatics while your emotions are being whisked up by a combination of lights, sounds and stage-play that leave you breathless (god I sound like Bruno Tonioli from Strictly Come Dancing). Out of all the incredible things I saw in Las Vegas, I think Cirque de Soliel was close to the peak.

By the way – the warning to my wife about it being naughty was justified. Zumanity was termed as a "Burlesque". To be honest, it would have been downright seedy if it wasn't for the wonderful acrobatic shows between the smutty and rather graphic dialogues from the Comperes as they were being set up. No top heavy luvlies here though – balance must be maintained at all times when you are an acrobat………

So that was Las Vegas.

A one-off place? - definitely. The Rome of modern times? Perhaps, though I don't see there being much of archaeological interest dug up here in the future.

It is worth visiting for the sheer audacity of the place and I **guarantee** that, no matter what your views are on places like this – you will not be able help enjoying yourself…..

Vegas had swept me up, thrown me about and left me tired but happy. However, next up was the Harley and the start of the real tour………

Chapter 2 – The Bike - Monster……

If you're reading this for the tour – well, this is where it starts….

"Hi All,
Now back online and can give you an update. If it is too boring then just
don't read it!

(very considerate of me eh?)

Was pretty harrowing getting started from Vegas. Arrived at Eagle
Rider at about 11am. Though I behaved the night before, still feeling a
little jaded by 4no., 20 hour days of madness…."

This was it – the start of the tour. I couldn't help but feel a little
nervous…., not helped by the fact that after being a little bit under the
Affluence of Incohol for four days, the mind finds it a little unusual to
be stone cold sober again. It says – wait a minute – something's not
right here…. a bit like my reaction to walking around the Venetian…..

The start of the adventure was difficult which I will describe shortly.
First though, a little about Bike Hire and what gear to bring.

Which Hire Company?

If you are contemplating doing a tour like this and you want to hire a
Harley – **it is not cheap.** If you accept this from the start you will save
yourself a lot of work and heartache. I began by getting a price from the
main ones that came up on an internet search and was shocked to find
that a decent sized bike was going to cost well over £100 per day (up to
$200 at the time). To put this into context, I found that I could hire a
Ford Mustang for the same price as a Harley which almost turned my
head (though the sun beating down on my face as I roared along the
desert roads with my Partick Thistle top on and Country Music drifting

up at me soon convinced me I had made the right decision....). If you find a company offering a cheaper deal, you will eventually find that either they won't let you drop the bike off at another location (absolutely necessary for a decent tour); or they haven't added on the cost of compulsory Insurance; or something similar. Whatever it is, it will take the price up over the £100 per day mark anyway.

Take it from me, unless things have changed drastically since writing this book, you'd be best not waste a load of time searching. After weeks emailing and calling every Bike-Hire Company I could find, I ended up back where I started – the largest and most high-profile one - Eagle Rider USA.

I would definitely recommend using a large company like Eagle Rider. They have outlets at most major Cities which makes planning your tour really easy. They offer good insurance and breakdown cover and they provide you with all the information you need when you start out. I'm sure a lot of the smaller Companies give out great information as well and they definitely offer more interesting and personal guided tours; but I had my whole tour planned out already and it was just nice to know that I could trust the hire Company to have a properly organised system behind me, just in case of problems.

As far as Insurance goes, they assume that you are already covered to actually ride a bike in the USA and then offer extra Insurance to cover the cost of the actual machine should you wreck it. You are also financially responsible for it if it is **stolen** so this extra Insurance is a must.

They typically offer three levels of cover depending on how much you want to be liable for if the bike is knackered or knicked. At the time I booked, you could insure yourself to only be liable for the first $1000 of the bike's value should it be stolen, for $24 per day. However, this cost would be reduced should you be happy to be liable for the first $2000 or the $3000 and so on.

I took option 1 – there's a lot of people out there who would like a Harley Electraglide.....

Which Bike?

This is tricky. I don't pretend to be an expert on Harleys or even motorcycles in general. At home I ride a souped-up 600 CC sport bike and only when work/kids/wife/guitar/time allows.

For me, riding around the USA meant it HAD to be a Harley. Harley Davidsons are just the Essence of Free, Big-Country USA and considering they are about as manoeuvrable as an Aircraft Carrier, they are well suited to the long, gently winding roads you find there (hmmm anyone would think they had actually designed them for this.....).

Harley Davidson have been building motor cycles since 1903. An interesting fact about them is how the HOG name (often used to describe Harleys) came about. Back in the 1920's Harley Davidson had motorcycle racing team who had a Piglet (a Hog) as a mascot. They were very successful and used to take the poor, frightened, leather-clad animal for victory laps after races. This is the origin of the name. Back in those days they weren't posh Formula One Types though. These guys were "rough-shod farm boys who would wipe out in one race, crack bones back into place, patch up the bike and be back on the grid for the next one". That is a quote from a very interesting article about them by "The Selvedge Yard" which you can find on the Tinterweb.

Back to bikes. It is easy to be seduced by the Custom Bikes. We all imagine ourselves as a character in Easy Rider, gliding along with a t-shirt on, feet and hands high in the air and the wind in our hair. Correspondingly, the first thing I looked at was the Custom bikes with massively fat back tyres and high bars and footrests..... aaaaahhhhh. However, these are out...... – they have no luggage capacity whatsoever......

The next option is the like of the Street Glide or Road King. These have reasonably large panniers and still look pretty-well cool. However, I looked at the Pannier Volume then did a bit of a take-off of all the gear, clothes and equipment I was taking. The conclusion was – with the panniers full, I would still need a fair-sized rucksack on my back. Now let's face facts; when you're cruising along and you see somewhere you want a closer look at, or a bar or restaurant to refuel yourself, you don't want to be climbing off the bike and wandering about with a huge rucksack on. Even if you take it off, you still then need to think about how you are going to lock it closed and then lock it to the bike.

(also the Desert necessitates something else riding on your back that we will encounter later)

So what are you left with? The Big Daddy of them all – the Electra-Glide. This bike has two panniers but also a back-box which can carry more than both panniers put together. They also lock reasonably securely which is a must. In the end I looked at the dimensions of the storage then got all my stuff together and assessed if it would all fit. This involved a bit of imagination without the actual boxes to pack the stuff in (my wife thought I was practicing a mime act….. again….) but it was all worth it in the end. When I came to pack up the bike after carting all my gear in a taxi from Vegas, it filled the storage completely but.... it all fit! This left me free to tour without a load of gear strapped to the bike or on my back.

The back box and panniers on an Electraglaide contain about 4.5 cubic feet of volume (approx 0.417m3). That doesn't sound like much but to put this in perspective, when I landed in Las Vegas I had a huge rucksack – completely full of everything from clothes, Kevlar Bike Jeans, full-face helmet, and so on; to eight T-shirts I had made up with a picture of my mate John "the Chef" draping his arm around the Chef from The Muppets while steam, smoke and god knows what else rises from the kitchen area (John's 40th was the reason we were all going to Vegas in the first place). I managed to fit all of this into the bike storage save the spare helmet which I stored by binding it to the pillion seat with some handy rubber straps I had brought.

What to bring?

What to bring depends greatly on where you are going. Any biker knows you have to plan for the weather but the extremes of weather on my tour were ridiculous. For example, it was about 40°C in Vegas and pushing towards 50°C in Death Valley so some Summer gear such as Kevlar open-mesh gloves were in order. However, the day after leaving the desert I would be passing through the Tioga Pass over the mountains of Yosemite which often doesn't open until late June after months and months of Snow clearing, In fact, as I was leaving for Las Vegas the pass still wasn't even open as they hadn't yet managed to punch through the last section from either side.... Hence, sub-zero bike gear was also required.

The main problem then - how to pack full Cold and Wet Weather Gear along with Hot Desert Gear – was solved by hiring the Electra-Glide.

Riding in the desert requires special care and I researched this quite a bit. I spent many an hour on motorcycle forums, taking advice from bikers who had been through Death Valley. Many had done it. Many had even done it in June/July as I was contemplating. However, not many had been daft enough to do it *alone* in June/July...... I took a lot of advice from them and from various official websites regarding safety. Understandably a lot of this was to do with staying hydrated. There is a lot of conflicting advice out there on dehydration when Desert-riding - some even advised that a gallon of water should be drank every half hour – a GALLON! I began to wonder how I would fit a rain barrel on the bike..... After a lot of thought, I decided that 50°C was just too much of a danger when biking alone. If the bike broke down I would be in serious bother very quickly. Those of you who have been through a desert will know that there is NO SHADE ANYWHERE and an hour or so in that heat...... It also became apparent later that the Bike Hire Company not only voids the Insurance if you go through Death Valley between May and September, but also won't come to get you in there if you break down..... "Aah. Mebbe's Naw then eh?"

On balance I decided it was best to go around Death Valley rather than through it.
However, even the route I took would have temperatures of well above 40°C so the danger remained. There were two main things that had to be adhered to:-

- Remain covered at all times. You need to keep that skin covered, not just so you don't burn but also because the wind is constantly against you on a bike, you don't realise the amount of sweat that is being evaporated from your bare skin as you ride along. This can lead to very sudden and unexpected dehydration. This is where the Kevlar Jeans come in. Many people had advised that full leathers should be worn even in the desert for safety in case of a spill. I decided that it would be so hot I would end up taking them off and then be completely unprotected. A compromise would be full length jeans with knee pads and Kevlar to hold them together if I came off to stop the denim melting into my arse as I skidded along the road..... I also took a Textile Bike Jacket rather than leather as I reckoned it would be cooler. These textile jackets are a lot cheaper than leather and some look pretty cool. The one I took was good enough to be worn out on the town which meant I didn't need to pack an extra jacket. When I got just too hot for the jacket, the long sleeved fitba (soccer) top would keep the top half completely covered. Also, any world-promotion of the mighty Partick Thistle (the best and only team in Glasgow.... cue losing most of the Scottish readers....) is a plus...

- Keep Hydrated and as Cool as possible. While on the forums I had a lot of people trying to sell me water filled vests. You can fill these with water (or even ice) every night and wear them under your shirt as you ride during the day to keep cool. This I didn't go for. However, I did go for a Hydration Pack which is an absolute must. You need to keep drinking water as you ride. If you don't, pretty soon you are going to start to feel a little light headed – which can very quickly lead on to serious dehydration. An internet search showed hydration packs (basically rucksacks that you fill with water with a drinking tube attached) were pretty bloody expensive. Also, it would be one more thing to carry over on the plane. However, I made a breakthrough – someone had had the brainwave of just developing a drinking tube that comes with a series of different bottle caps that would fit any water bottle commonly on sale. What a brilliantly simple idea – the Inventor must have been a Scot (hey we invented TV, Golf, the Steam Engine, the Light Bulb, Caffiene-filled and super strong tonic wine and the Alka Seltzer........ Ok I made the last one up but the only reason we didn't is because a lot of us don't like to sober up long enough to have a hangover......). I tried this contraption out on various bottles and it worked a treat. This meant that I could use a very small rucksack for general use, then, by sticking a couple of 1.5 litre bottles in it, it would become a hydration pack for the desert. If you are a keen walker, snowboarder, skier or mountain biker this is a useful piece of kit and can be bought from the Tinterweb for about £8 – look up "SmarTube".

I won't bore you with the full list of gear I took with me but here are the important bits:-

- **A Full Face Helmet**. The bike hire companies give you an open face helmet which is great for the heat. However, as my mate Michael advises "a chin is a nice thing to have" so I took my own full face for the more dangerous areas such as the Freeway (oh Christ the Freeway into L.A.. I don't even want to think about it) and the colder sections of my route.
- **Bike Boots that could double up as dress shoes on nights out** – I tell you these were hard to find. The ones I eventually got were black leather and pretty cool-looking in a Chelsea-Boot kind of way. What's more, they came with a wee elasticised leather scuff band that you could stick over your left boot while riding so the gear pedal didn't ruin them. Cool or not, I have a feeling that these may have been women's boots (it would certainly explain why the mincing sales assistant was

winking at me so much....) but there you go – most bikers don't need to carry gear with them dressy enough to get them into a Las Vegas club....

- **Kevlar Jeans** as described above. These again were cool enough to wear in social situations if need-be (and by social I of course mean the Boozer)

- **Mesh, Summer Bike Gloves** and **Full Winter Bike Gauntlets** too. Unavoidable.

- **A cycle lock and a snowboard lock**. As I had my whole world in the back box of the bike, I took a reasonably hefty cycle lock with me which I looped right over the top of the back box as an extra layer of security when I wasn't around. A snowboard lock is a really handy little gadget. A palm sized plastic housing with a two-foot long, wound-steel wire which can be pulled out, looped around things then plugged back in to a combination lock. This was used to lock the full-face helmet to the bike when I was wearing the chin-grater version.

- **Textile Bike Jacket** as described above.

- **A Back Protector**. These fit on under your jacket and stop your spine getting snapped among other things if you come off. I needed one for snowboarding trips and had found a decent one to be about £200. However, I bought the same one from a Biker Supplies Store on the Tinterweb for £50 – Wintersports Snobbishness versus bikers down-to-earth value eh?

- **A Rucksack without a frame.** This is a very important detail! I just remembered in time that the rucksack I would use to carry all my gear on the plane and so on, had to fold up and go in the bike panniers later – phew…

Chapter 3 - The Desert

Majestic, Beautiful..... BAD-ASS

This was the Start of the Journey

What with the heat, the soberishness, and the fact that the bike was a monster – I didn't get very far at first.......:-

> *"This was it – the start of the tour. I couldn't help but feel a little nervous as I was dropped at Eagle Rider....*
>
> *Once all the rigmarole was done I had to try to fit all my gear, including the rucksack and spare helmet, onto the bike. Good preparation turned out to be the key as the extra locks and elastics brought from home were the clincher. The problem was that it was already about 100 degrees and by the time I had found a way to fit it all in, the sweat was running off of me in rivers.*
>
> *The bike is **HUGE**. With all the extra weight I had added in the back box (making it really top-heavy), I found that I had to drive it around the building about 8 times just to try to sort out my balance. It is so heavy that you have to be very careful to get your lean just right when you turn. Also, when at a standstill if it leans just ever so slightly to one side, you need all your might to get it back up again. (Doing this in shorts without burning your legs on the engine is quite a feat - not always accomplished...).*
>
> *Eventually, I left the parking lot. Went 2 miles and stopped at McDonalds to cool off......."*

Ahhhh McDonalds….. – that great bastion of the modern American way of life with its air conditioning, ubiquitous menu and friendly welcome….. Some people may think I am being sarcastic here but McDonalds has saved my life on many forays into deepest, darkest

Eastern Europe with the Tartan Army. Try showing up in Moldova, exhausted and starving after 16 hours of travelling, not a clue what all the signs say as they are all in Cyrillic, no idea where your hotel is and no restaurants or fast food outlets anywhere..... (this is Moldova where there is a communist government and no public or private money floating around whatsoever). It's kind of scary. Then you see those Golden Arches shining out through the dark............ "Oh Thank ####!" is the universally accepted exclamation in these situations.

This case was no exception. I was struggling to balance the bike, I was getting pretty dehydrated already (having spent so long packing it up) and I needed some time out. Good old Mickey D's!
I made the mistake of ordering a LARGE meal, forgetting that I was in the States – this turned out to be larger than a Supersize meal in Scotland. Come one guys – give yourselves at least a chance of staying slim…. However, it sorted me right out. I had a look at the map and went for the desert……

"When I plucked up courage to carry on, I just couldn't get onto the highway. I kept getting in the wrong lane, missing turnings and so on. All the stops at traffic lights were in 100 degree-heat which, coupled with the stress of the situation, was putting me in a dehydrated mess all over again. However, planning to the rescue - I had attached my drinking tube to a large bottle of water prior to starting. The desert is not a forgiving place....

After a full hour I finally got on to highway 95 and headed north to the edge of Death Valley.

I found with massive pleasure that the radio on a Harley works superbly and is actually, really clear when riding. I found a Country-Music Station and headed off into the desert with much ridiculous whooping and shouts of "Vegas Baby!" and other similar expressions I seemed to have picked up…..

I skirted the edge of Death Valley and it was hot, hot, hot – the bikes thermometer said 120 and whenever I stopped, I almost melted. The roads in the desert are long and straight, the scenery is burnt and severe but then..... strangely beautiful..... At the time, the only words I could muster up in my head to describe it were..... "Majestic" and "Bad-Ass!". Driving in the desert is like the video to the song "Stylo" by Gorilla's. You're hammering along the endless straight roads, looking ahead to the shimmering horizon, then suddenly a real muscle car roars past you like in this video – real Vegas-mobiles like Chevrolet Camaros, Ford Mustangs and sometimes those ridiculous car/pickup mixtures with massive engines and really no practical use at all. You think, "who the hell is in there and what are they all about?"

The desert really is a beautiful place. At first you think it all looks the same, as you are slowly hypnotised by the massively wide-open spaces and the long straight road stretching to the horizon and beyond. Then you start to notice the detail as you pass some palm trees or some rock faces burnt a different colour - solitary, sparse beauty. However, you are also constantly thinking about the power of the place. If you were to venture out into these wide-open spaces you would be dead pretty quickly – only the hardiest of animals and plant life survives. You realise that, in spite of all of our technology, Mother Nature can be hugely powerful and she needs to be respected. Hence, my wonderfully eloquent description – Majestic, Beautiful.... BADASS! (Laurence Olivier? 'mon oo-er and ah'll gie yoo a few pointurrs mate).

When the sun starts to go down it adds another aspect. Shadows from any rocky outcrops race across the desert and the rocks seem to turn a redder shade, changing the whole look of the place.

"I was also struck by the odd building sitting completely on its own in the desert, far away from the main road, with a neon sign saying something like "Gentleman's Club". Hmmm curious....

Yes, there are places of entertainment even in the middle of the Mojave Desert. To be honest they are strange sights. You have seen nothing but desert for 50 miles, then, all of a sudden there is a building with a huge Neon sign, out in the middle of it. Talk about not wanting to annoy the neighbours.......

Desert.....desert...... desert...... strange building far off...... desert..... desert......

On closer inspection.
Bikinis Gentlemen's Club.
"Actually I saw one today, really about 50 miles from any shaded place, called "The Shady Lady Ranch", which on passing inspection appeared to be a small wooden shack with a trailer and some rusted old cars around it. Mmmm enticing....."

I believe this was The Shady Lady Ranch. Nice!

"Anyway. I ran out of water and within <u>minutes</u> was feeling light headed. One of the scary things in the desert is there are hardly any signs at all so you never know where you are. And believe me, there is absolutely NO shade. There isn't even anywhere to stop. Cars can manage to pull onto the soft shoulder but I can't as the bike will sink and if the stand sinks into the ground, I struggle to get the bike upright again."

That's true you know. I couldn't even stop. The verge to the road is gravel and the ridiculously small stand on the Electra Glide just sinks straight down into it - which led to an episode later.

"Rather than mother you like we do in Britain, I think here if you go out into the desert, you are expected to be prepared enough to make it through.
After a fair old ride, my water supply suddenly dried up. I was pretty sure I was nearly at Beatty as I had looked up the mileage before leaving Vegas (I had more water stowed on the bike by the way) and sure enough, I came around the corner and saw the sprawling

metropolis of Beatty where I was staying. As it seemed to me, Beatty consisted of a gathering of wooden buildings, trailers and the odd motel - basically an old prospecting village. It was so hot I was ready for "keeling ower" so found my motel (surprisingly nice) and lay in the air-conditioned room for so long I had to put a jumper on!"

Beatty is not a big town. It seemed reasonably sizeable when I was booking a hotel on the internet but when I came over the hill I really wondered if I was in the right place. There were wooden shacks, the obligatory garage (the like of which you see in every movie based in the desert) with trestle tables set out in front covered with old, rusty car parts for sale - and that was about it. I was struggling a bit with the heat now and stopped in front of the trestle tables to ask where the hotel was.

The old, cracked-face guy with the sideways tractor cap who I asked for directions made a lot of "aaayyaa, oiaaaarr and thaaarr" noises and I didn't understand a word of it save the "boy!" at the end...... I got back on the bike.

After I came to the only crossroads, complete with a single hanging traffic light (just like in the Disney Pixar film - "Cars"), I turned right and passed a real-life, old-time, timber, saloon; a trailer park and straight after that an Army-Surplus open-air "market". Then I came to the hotel..... and do you know what? It was modern, clean, and....... Air-Conditoned... aaaaahhhh.
It seems that every small town in the States has either a Motel 8 or a Motel 6 (it's cheaper little brother). *Tripadvisor* is full of people complaining about these hotels saying things like "The towels were thin.".................. I mean...... "The Towels were thin"!! Get a bloody life!!!. I found these places to be exactly what it says on the tin: clean, functional, and modern - kind of how you would expect a Travelodge to be in Britain.

It is incredible though how gambling is involved in everything in Nevada. Right next to the hotel in this tiny, desert town was a reasonably large, modern casino, packed with all manner of gaming machines, gaming tables, a bar or two..... and, absolutely no customers - not one.

Oh, and next door to that was the strangest petrol station I have ever seen........

A wee bit of History.

Beatty was founded at about the same time as Las Vegas and, like Vegas, was originally a source of water. Montillius Beatty bought the Lander Ranch in 1896 and, being one of only three white men in the area (everyone else was Shoshone or Paiute Indian - including his wife) welcomed all travellers into his home. In 1904 a couple of guys called

Shorty and Ed passed through and, plied with some "Ol' Be Joyful" Whisky, let slip that they had found Gold! This generated a little interest as you can imagine and sparked one of the largest (and shortest) Gold Rushes in the history of the Nevada Area. We'll come back to this...

Soon after, in 1904, another prospector called Robert Montgomery purchased a section of the ranch from Mr Beatty and founded the town, named after ole' Montillius himself. There were several towns in the area but (like Vegas) Beatty could provide water which helped it rise in importance very quickly.

With the arrival of the railway and roads being built between Beatty and neighbouring towns, it quickly became the Hub of travel and supply for all the towns in the area. This was just as well for them as the Gold Rush was a flash in the pan.....

Robert Montgomery founded the main Gold Mine in the area - the Montgomery Shoshone Mine - about 5 miles away. The Gold Rush was so intense that another town was founded there just three months after Beatty - the town of Rhyolite.

This town is the classic story of American over-exuberance....... The town began its life in early 1905. Beatty, the main hub in the area, never had more than around 650 inhabitants throughout its entire history. By contrast, a mere two years after it was founded, Rhyolite had somewhere between 3500 and 5000 people in it! It is said to have had a Hospital, a School, a Stock Exchange and even an Opera House of sorts.....

Then, by 1911 - a mere 6 years after it was founded - the mine had closed and the inhabitants had dwindled to 1000. By 1920 the town was deserted and soon became famous again...... as a Ghost Town...... It has been the setting for several films since then and was also the setting for a rather spooky episode for me.....

Beatty did it's best to stay as important as it could through the years but by 1942, the Railroad had been torn up by the War Office for use during World War Two. Beatty had to rely on road users then. At this point I add a little conjecture - what do tired road users want?......... Bikinis Gentleman's Club! Talk about enterprising...

....

"Later, when it had cooled down a little (almost a whole 2 degrees) I went out on the bike again. Had heard there was a ghost town nearby called Rhyolite.....
I was on the bike in shorts and t-shirt and, while I was cruising down a hill, I saw something lying in the road. It looked like it was a strip of something which had fallen off of a truck. I made to avoid it, just catching the end, and it wasn't until I was running over the end of it that I realised it was a bloody great snake! The head whipped up and I could hear it hissing at me even over the racket of the engine."

Desert, shorts, snake. Brilliant! "Ya Wee Hissin' Bastat!"

"Next I turned up to the ghost town. It wasn't very impressive. A few old buildings (much of the place was ransacked for building materials once it was deserted) but there was the odd, abandoned pre-war vehicle there which lent the place a bit of character and allowed the mind to imagine how things were..... but as the sun was going down, it was a little spooky. Nothing is as silent as the desert - no human life, no birds, no wind, nothing. Put this together with a lot of abandoned buildings and it gives a bit of a shiver..."

The desert really is bloody quiet. It was strange as the sun went down, the shadows raced across the ground and the rocks glowed a sort of red. Everything was soundless. And then....

"Just down the track is one of those surreal things that only pop up in the strangest of places. A Belgian artist had created all these ghostly figures from fibreglass, presented in various situations..... and then for some reason sited them smack in the middle of the desert, near a disused mining town, miles from anywhere......."

These things are freaky. Shrouded, ghostly figures stooping over bicycles or the like. With the silence of the desert, I started to get a little chill....

"One of them is called the last supper. Conjure up an image of Death in your mind - Death the person - basically a sort of hooded shroud and nothing else. That's what they are all like. The last supper is a group of them together (I imagine to represent Jesus and the A-Fruit-Pastilles) and all in the middle of the desert - why?
I was wandering around looking at these things in deathly silence and got a bit spooked. Suddenly a well-lit bar with a raucous juke box and some top-heavy luvlies in the corner seemed more inviting than ever. I went over to the bike and - guess what - the stand had sunk into the ground and it was nearly over. After a couple of tries I was beginning to think I would not be able to lift it at all and would be stuck there for the night with all the silent ghouls.... This actually scared the drawers off of me and I suddenly found the strength to lift it"

(Am I just weak? How do people deal with an Electra-Glide that's tipped over. It would be easier to slide a whale doon the beach without bursting it....)

"Thankfully I got there in the end, rewarded with several nice engine-burns. I quickly went and dropped the bike at the hotel and wandered down to the saloon with a relieved spring in my step - nothing cheers a man up like a near-spooked-experience followed by the promise of beers, bars and beauties."

Imagine this in deathly silence with desert all around as far as the eye can see.....

If you look carefully you can make out the bike in the background, gradually sinking into the gravel......

I was really looking forward to hitting a real, Wild-West, Desert Saloon. However, it was a bit of a let-down. I imagined a few rough old cowboys hanging over the bar, some Daisy-Duke girls playing pool and Toby Keith drifting out of the juke box. It certainly looked like that sort of place from the outside.... However,

"I love being in with the locals and usually people want to talk to you but this place was different. A few trailer-livers; a couple of young Mexicans - complete with moustaches like Lee Van Cleef; an obvious farmer's boy and a cowboy-hatted old bloke who was just like Patrick Swayze's old ex-bouncer mate in the film "Roadhouse".
This would normally have been bleedin' excellent for some craic, however, none of them were interested in chatting with me - they were all polite but that was it. Soon I realised that it was a good thing as every person seemed to want to be the centre of attention all the time...... just without anything to actually say at all. If in doubt, just SHOUT IT OUT!"

However, the evening was saved in some fine style by a rather amusing sign I found in the toilets:-

"Please do not put cigarette butts down the urinal. The hands that pick them out are the same hands that put the ice cubes in your drink."

Ok not the most amusing platitude I'd ever heard but what was great was that someone had actually gone to the trouble of *hand-engraving* this into an old looking square of metal to hang it on the wall.

I also noted something that seems to be quite normal in USA.... and freaks me out! As a (grudging) European, I can't imagine going for a number 2 while a complete stranger goes for a number 1 right beside you! Noooooooo........

Ok, you could probably have locked the door to the whole toilet there but I have been in many others where you can't. Sometimes one wall can consist of: urinal; urinal; urinal; urinal; toilet pan....... No Way!

Anyway, that was the highlight of what looked like would be a cool place from the outside:-

I wrote "Mark Guitar Curtis fae Glasgow - On the Jags!" on a dollar bill, stapled it to the wall and left.

Please note - I sound like a Free-riding Rebel doing this - stapling a bit of self-indulgent history onto peoples' drab, desert lives in an act of wanton vandalism..........
I suppose I need to reluctantly point out that a lot of other people had already done this and I was just timidly adding to it...
If you ever by chance pass through Beatty, Nevada, go and find my Dollar Bill and add one next to it - hey, in ten years we might have 3 Dollars!....

"Tuesday - Up early and ran a couple of miles at 8am to avoid the heat - big mistake."

Have you ever seen a boiled egg, dripping in engine oil? Well that was mah heid when I got back.

Once I recovered I went for a quick wander - today was going to be a big day - 210 miles of mainly open desert, turning to Redwoods and mountains later on. The route I was on from Las Vegas to Yosemite was taking me along the Western boundary of the giant Nellis Air Force

Range. This houses (among other things) the Tonopah Test Range and, not too far from Beatty, the infamous Groom Lake - also known as "Area 51"...... As you probably know, this is an area of great secrecy and even greater conspiracy theory which I will come to shortly. However, as I walked around Beatty I found some absolutely shameless marketing, taking advantage of the proximity to these places of intrigue. How about the "Space Station Market! - Cigarettes, Beer, Wine and Alcohol". Perhaps I'm being picky but aren't wine and beer alcohol too? Or the "Area-51 RV Park!" (basically a dodgy-looking caravan park). Both of these class establishments had signs adorning pictures of Drones and Alien-looking Military Craft as if that had something to do with the normality within.... Americans can make money out of ANYTHING - fair play to them.

There was also a large area at the side of the road selling "surplus army gear". Basically, this seemed to consist of.......... Ammo crates........... Just ammo crates......... A vast number of ammo crates. They were spread out over the whole area; some small enough to have had rifle rounds in; some large enough to have housed missiles. With passing trade of about 4 cars an hour, this was just weird.....

Yes, Beatty was a little strange all in all, well worth a visit but a little strange. However, eager to be on my way, I saddled up my 1.7 litre, black and shiny steed and headed out into the open desert.....

Nellis Air Force Range

This is a giant area (recently re-named the **Nevada Test and Training Range)** controlled by the Military which houses many Air Force Bases and research facilities. Near to Tonopah is the Tonopah Test Range (or "Area 52") which is a testing area for Classified Military Aircraft. There are pictures all over the internet of strange drones that people have seen from outside this area. There are certainly plenty of signs on that side of the Highway 95 telling of "Patrolling Aircraft" and some strange looking Radio Beacons, but the only unusual activity I saw was a helicopter (that looked suspiciously like "Airwolf") hammering around kicking up dust on a hillside.

However, to the South-East of this is Groom Lake,....... or **Area 51**. Most people have heard of this place from conspiracy theory based films like X-Files and so on. Conspiracy theories aside, this place is definitely housing some secret activities.

The American Government did not even acknowledge the *existence* of a base at Groom Lake until 2003. It had gone to great lengths to keep the place off the map – at the time of writing, it is not shown on any Public Government Maps at all. It isn't shown on official Aeronautical Aviation Charts either which show Groom Lake itself but not the Airport Base. These just classify the restricted area as part of the "Nellis Range Restricted Area". This restriction is taken seriously - even Military Pilots training in the Nellis Range are apparently subject to "disciplinary action" if they enter the airspace around Groom Lake.

Satellite images of the area taken in the 1960's by the Corona Spy Satellite have since been de-classified but the area of Groom Lake is mysteriously missing from them. The Government was still removing Satellite images as recently as 2004 when they removed "Terra" images from Microsoft's "Terraserver-USA". The thing I find quite ridiculous however is that you can zoom right in on both the Tonopah Test Range and the base at Groom Lake on Google Earth - just type in "Groom Lake, Nevada" and suddenly you're looking right at it! It seems that the satellite imagery that is often removed is a lot higher resolution than that found on Google but still, it just shows you how wide-open the world has become over the last decade or so......

Conspiracy Theorists tend towards Area 51 housing evidence of Alien life or even Alien Weaponry. It seems more plausible that the base is used for the development of new aircraft or aircraft weapons systems. These would obviously be kept under strict secrecy until they reached a stage where production was likely. Then it would make sense that they be transferred to Area 52 for more extensive testing and training.

From a tourists' point of view though, Area 51 is guarded by private security contractors who ride around the range in Humvees and pickups. They are armed but apparently tend to warn people off and then follow them until the County Sheriff arrives, rather than engage them in anything more sinister. Brandish a camera though and you might find yourself looking down at your ankles with your hands behind your back with a nice M16 at your temple….. I met a few people on my trip who reckoned they had taken the route to Area 51 and suddenly encountered a group of Humvees appearing over the hills when they got past the warning signs - this could be quite a fun tourists trip.....!

One last thing - if you look around the area to the West of Highway 95 on Google Earth or the like; you will see some strange, huge, green circles in the middle of the desert (just type in **37.69083N, 118.0775W** into the "Fly to" box if you can't find them). When you see them immediately you think of crop circles and mysterious military projects. I'll leave it to you to track down what these are - something a lot less sinister.....

"Opted for open fronted shirt and shorts and factor 25 - just too bloody hot."

Ok so I shed the Textile Jacket. Excessive heat has a way of making you throw caution to the wind when you need to cool down. However, I kept the back protector on along with the bike boots and the summer bike-gloves (but if I'm totally honest these were just to look cool........... see below)

Check the desert view in the mirror too.

"About 10 miles into the desert I found the Cruise Control! Now the long, straight, ridiculously wide roads are even easier! Get up to 65 or 70, apply the cruise and relax. Take photos, listen to the radio.

These roads are long and straight. The sun beats down, the country music drifts up, the desert gradually hypnotises you with its sparse beauty and with Cruise Control you can just drift away and enjoy it.

("Excuse me Mr Curtis but we believe that to be a very irresponsible attitude to controlling a motorised perambulator and it should not be promoted to the general proletariat!"
"Aww cam-oan Auld-Yin! It's no like there a loat tae dae!")

"Eventually you get to the stage where you see a corner coming about 8 or 9 miles ahead and you think "uh-oh. Corner coming - need to concentrate" and you start preparing yourself......"

Every 50 miles or so I would pass through a small village or town - legacies of the Gold Rush. I stopped for a break in "Goldfield" and it was hotter than an Arab's sand-shoe..... There was very little to see though I spotted a Petrol Station with a sign saying "Weird Beer Here!". These places were quiet. It was so hot that as a Scotsman (used to the occasional dry day in midsummer) I just couldn't see how people could function doing normal everyday jobs in heat like that. While I was standing gradually melting, a siren started and a very large Fire Engine emerged from a nearby building. God, how I felt for the blokes inside in all the fireproof gear! Desert life breeds tough people....

After Tonopah Route 95 changes to Route 6 and I veered off from going North to head West towards the Sierra Nevada Mountains. It was still desert and still outrageously hot. However, soon I found a surreal sight, snow peaked mountains in the distance across the desert. There was also (finally!) the odd place to stop. These rest areas were purpose-built and irrigated so that trees could grow and what do trees provide? SHADE! AAaaahhhh shade. Never felt so glad of it.

Now I was heading for a town called **Bishop** - this was to the East side of the mountains and would allow me to cross them through the Yosemite National Park the next day. Anyone considering crossing the desert and then Yosemite, I would heartily recommend cutting off of Route 6 and on to Route 120 - this is a small turnoff at a tiny village called **Bennet**. The reason I would recommend this is the sudden, in fact almost immediate way the desert changes into something else – something greener with crazy-looking rock formations and huge trees.

"Eventually I turned onto a minor road and found myself climbing into a different country. I stopped to take pics (actually, I also stopped to set camera up and take video of myself riding by like in the film "Bad News"!)."

I am so vain it is ridiculous. You have all seen films where the star is driving down the freeway/motorway and you see lots of camera shots of the car cruising by. Well the reality of this was brought home to me by the tongue-in-cheek documentary made about a fictional Rock Band called "Bad News" (Rik Mayall, Adrian Edmondson, Nigel Planer and Peter Richardson). They are on their way to a gig when the Interviewer, who is in the van with them, asks the Singer when they will arrive there. He responds that "It would be a lot sooner if we didn't have to keep letting the camera crew out at every bridge to film us driving by......." Well I wanted a shot of myself roaring by on the Harley so I found a secluded, long, straight, side road with a signpost on it. I climbed up the signpost and clamped my camera to the top. Without a remote-control I had to just start it filming and leave it running until I could retrieve it. The plan was to roar away, go far enough for it not to see me turning around, then ride past it as though it was part of my journey. I would then clip it later. Yes, I am obsessed with recording every part of everything I do. This is partly extreme vanity but also partly due to a lack of confidence in my useless memory...... and also partly due to a lack of confidence in my useless memory...... :-)

Anyway, I carried out this process and have never cut the film up as it was so funny the way it ended up. The film begins: I climb down; get on the bike and roar away. Then there is a 2-minute period of total silence as the bike gradually dwindles away into the distance. Then there is a 1 minute period of nothing at all. Then there is another 2-minute period where the bike gradually reappears and gets closer. Then there is about <u>half a second</u> of great film as I roar by at great speed going "AAaaaarrrggghhh!!!". All that build-up for such a tiny reward. My wife says this is a familiar scenario but I don't know what she means.........

Anyway, back to the story and the reason for taking the turn-off at Bennet.

"Started back on the road - it was windy which was a welcome challenge after the straight roads of the desert - then 3 things happened really quickly:-

- firstly, I started seeing some green aside from the cactuses for the first time in 2 days;
- then, all of a sudden (and I mean all of a sudden), I was into Redwoods. What a massive change - It happened so quickly that I thought I must have dropped off and gone 20 miles on Autopilot. These pine trees really are red. Their bark is a dark, rusty red that contrasts beautifully with the dark green foliage. It is really pretty.

- then I rode over a ridge and suddenly there it was........ The Sierra Nevada and Yosemite! (no not "Sam", the other Yosemite). Hundred miles of the Sierra Nevada snowy mountains stretching in a North/South line - and here I was still on the edge of the desert in 100 degree plus heat..."

This was some sight and the fact that it all happened so quickly made it all the more awesome. It took my breath away and was the start of two days of absolute jaw-dropping beauty. I would really recommend this route and the subsequent "Juniper Loop" for anyone thinking of crossing the mountains from the desert.

"What's more, giant Mono Lake appeared down to my right - crystal blue and stretching-out for miles."

If you look at the map you will see Mono Lake to the East of the mountains at the Tioga Pass leading into Yosemite. Mono is huge (at some 760 square miles) and is a Terminal Lake which means it has no outlet to the Ocean. Because of this, there is a huge concentration of dissolved salt in it which makes the water extremely alkaline and saline. However, what I liked was the beauty of this huge, indigo area suddenly appearing after the monochrome of the desert. The redwoods around it on the Route 120 side are sparse enough to give a great view in between them. I'm not sure you would want to swim in it though - it has 4 to 6 trillion Brine Shrimp within it throughout the summer months that are no bigger than your thumbnail; and the indigenous people of the area used to derive their nutrition from the larvae of the Alkaline Flies that swarm there..... mmmmmmm.

June Lake Loop

I have mentioned Lonely Planet several times in this book. Here, again it provided me with a fantastic route to take.
After passing Mono Lake, route 120 eventually meets the main Highway that runs North/South up the East side of the Sierra Nevada Mountains - Highway 395, better known as "Three Flags Highway".

Now from here I could have just gone straight South for about 70 miles to **Bishop**. However, I had taken a quick flick through L.P. before I left in the morning and it mentioned the **June Lake Loop** which was just off of this road. If it hadn't I would have ridden straight past the sign. I leaned the bike around some windy roads through the redwoods then was struck by a sight.

"Imagine, you come over the top of a hill and there below is a crystal blue lake, with green all around it, which gradually turns to grey rock as you work your way up to the white snow of the mountain behind it. Just stunning!..."

This is actually really impressive. June Lake is in a dip, well below the level of the Highway, but has the awesome Sierra Nevada mountain range towering straight up behind it. We have all seen emerald-blue water on holiday somewhere exotic. However, here you look down on the beautiful blue water but you see the reflection of the grey, white-capped mountains towering straight up behind it. With the sun glittering on the water it gives the effect of a sparkling mountain range. Quite fantastic! (am I overselling this?).

"Went down, parked up the Harley and sat with my feet in the water eating a HUGE bag of American hot crisps – fat?... Who .... Me?"

It was a rather relaxing hour I spent there. There are camp sites all around June Lake so it would be a cracking spot to spend the night before tackling Yosemite and the mountains the next day. However, I had decided on a town with a nice Hotel in it.

"From there it was a long drive down to Bishop where I was staying, listening to country music and watching my arms slowly burn..."

*"Roared into Bishop and found the Ramada Motel - absolute luxury after last night. It is like a motel you see in the movies – terraced rooms with a walkway along the front - kind of like the ones you imagine you can rent by the hour....., but being Ramada it is WELL posh. However, I turned up in a white, open necked t-shirt – totally **yellow** from sweat; jean-shorts that were nothing short of filthy; and legs covered in road kill – the receptionist nearly keeled over."*

It's quite amazing what gets stuck to your legs when riding in shorts - the massive bugs are only the start. Once you've been sprayed with blood from running over road kill and then melted bitumen from the roadworks, it makes for an interesting shell of gruesome armour. My appearance sorely tested the famous American welcome. She passed the test though, but only just with a smile stretched tighter than a Vegas Dancers' top.

"By the time I got in, showered and back out it was 9pm and all the restaurants were shut. Walking up and down Main St., I found a small

bar - blaring music and with about 10 very rowdy locals in it. So of course I went in......"

Yes this bar was pretty wild for a Wednesday night. However, I ought to have known...

*"Had a beer or two then realised that the 3 noisy guys down the bar were **Scottish** -here I am, in a tiny bar in a small mountain-edge town and I meet 3 blokes from Stirling!"*

I might have known - we like a drink and a laugh us Jocks...

"They were doing much the same tour as me but in a Dodge Challenger - style!"

"Once they left I started playing a game called "shuffle" with the locals - one of whom kept going on that he was a true Indian. He went on and on about it so I eventually showed him what it meant to be a true Scotsman!"

Should I provide a translation here for the English and the rest of the planet? - hmmm I think not. Let's just say it gets a bit breezy with a kilt on.

"Anyway, this "Shuffle" game was basically sliding pucks up a special board and seemed to be based on the game people used to play on ships that you see in paintings of Victorian nautical scenes. Went on to cuff the lot of them at it. Scotland!

Gave a guy called "Austin" a hard time for thinking I was Irish then proceeded to ask him where I could get fed at this time of night. Luckily he wasn't too annoyed and told me..."

Here's a bit of advice to anyone going anywhere in the U.S. for a holiday. If you want something to eat and everywhere is shut - ask where the local "Dinny's" is. This is a chain of sort of Mexican themed restaurants and they are open 24 hours. A quality burger with salad, some Mexican specialities, a great breakfast, all available 24 hours a day. Helped me out no end.

Mixing with the locals - perfect end to a good day."

- - - - - - - - - - - - - - - - - -

Chapter 4 - The Mighty Yosemite

"John Muir hud his Heid screwed oan"

I just can't tell you enough about how Yosemite surprised me, amazed me, and filled me with awe. I knew a little bit about it from the John Muir Museum that we casually meandered into when camping at a little seaside village near Edinburgh called Dunbar, but that was it.

John Muir

John Muir was a boy who lived in this little seaside village near Edinburgh in the mid 1800's. He had a very hard and strict upbringing by his father who was devoted to the Presbyterian Church. His father believed that anything outside of work that didn't involve bible studies was frivolous and punishable. Hence the work was never-ending and free time was scarce. We read about John Muir occasionally getting the special treat of a potato for his supper.... and no doubt a nice punishment beating to go with it.

John Muir was taken to America by his family when he was 11. British and Irish people had been emigrating to America since the 1600's. In Scotland it was thought that a person, stuck in their lowly position in the British Class System, could work their way into a better position in society in America. There was rich prairie-land to farm there and what's more; those without money could have their passage to America paid-for by Employers in return for working for them for a period of often 7 years. Immigration from Britain and Ireland increased massively in the 1840's partly due to the Irish Potato Famine, and John Muir was taken across in the middle of this huge influx. In our time, if you are told by *Lastminute.com* that a resort in the Costa Brava is "full of life and vitality" and then, when you get there you find it is a building site; you can just go home..... In John Muir's time, after a couple of months on a boat (if you were lucky enough to have Steam Power to accompany the sails) carrying all the meagre possessions you have left in the world, you had to make the best of it when you got there, no matter what.....

Basically, from then on John Muir spent around 14 hours a day working for his father trying to establish a farm. However, it is said that he would often get up at 1am to spend 4 hours before work, devoting time to his greatest pleasures - reading and inventions. The man was driven.....

In 1868 Muir travelled to the Sierra Nevada Mountains and was captivated by the Yosemite Valley. He returned there the following year to work as a Shepherd and then in a Sawmill, and began writing papers about the area which were published in such places as the New York Tribune. Over the next 6 years, John Muir began a movement to conserve the area in its natural form which led to the formation of the Yosemite National Park in 1890. He also founded a conservation movement called "The Sierra Club" which has grown to be one of the largest conservation movements in America today. We didn't appreciate just how important John Muir is to American Culture and Conservation when we were in Dunbar. He is a massive name in America and all this from a wee lad from East of Edinburgh.

When you see the old black and white picture of Muir, standing on top of a mountain with President Teddy Roosevelt; read the caption which says that Roosevelt told all advisors that he was not to be disturbed for three days while being taken around Yosemite by Muir; and then remind yourself that he was just a wee lad from Dunbar.... it is quite incredible. I have really enjoyed learning about this big fella and could write an awful lot more......

Wednesday - The Tioga Pass

"Today I tackled the Tioga pass – the road that runs right over the top of the Seirra Nevada and through John Muir's Yosemite National Park.

Once again sights that are just astounding."

"After a brief fling with fuel related terror (nearly ran out in the middle of no-where) I made it to the foot of the mountains again. This time sweltering in full bike gear."

The Tioga pass (otherwise known as Highway 120) runs right across the mountains from East to West. As it does so, it runs right through the centre of Yosemite National Park. It is hard to believe when you are riding through the Fiery Desert to get here, that it may not even be open yet due to Snow. They start clearing the snow along the route in mid-April - working their way in from either end simultaneously. Often, they don't meet in the middle until late May, sometimes well into June!

This road is just a must if you have to cross the mountains. The alternative route to the South of the mountains takes you from Las Vegas to L.A. and is quicker. But it really just consists of Freeway through desert-land. The sights you see while driving the Tioga Pass are the type that you would have to hike for days to see anywhere else in the world. The Americans do this kind of thing right for tourists - the money they must have spent not only to create this road in the location that it is in, but also to maintain it, must be huge.

"At this time of year Yosemite seems to have 3 seasons. It is summer at the bottom with rocks, trees, greenery, sparkling lakes, etc. all around you.

However, as you climb up it becomes spring – with bursting rivers and waterfalls from the snow melt.

Then at the top it is still winter - snow, ice, fantastic Winter scenes like frozen, snow-covered lakes with crystal-blue water showing through here and there."

However, the best thing about this road is this: the Tioga pass goes up and down, taking you from one season to another as you go….. Summer, to Spring, to Winter, to Spring, to Winter again, to Spring and so on....

"First – the climb. Going up winding roads that seem to have been sliced into the side of the mountains – Lorraine you would HATE this."

(my wife is scared of heights and gave me a HUGE amount of ear-ache just for making here drive up to the Aviemore Ski Resort car park to pick me up once....)

"However, as you go along you come to incredible white and blue lakes. The white is the still frozen and snow covered part. The sun beats down on the thawed parts and turns the water crystal blue."

Frozen Lake

Shades of "The Blue Oyster Bar" n'est pas?

*"Driving along the top of the mountains takes you to massive torrents of water from the snow melt above, then up into the snow, then down again. I stopped a few times just to take it in. The water is a deep bluey-green flowing not just in the rivers, but through the forested areas, in amongst and between the trees too at a tremendous rate. There are huge glades of green interspersed with lavender flowers and blue water making them absolutely beautiful (Coming Out?.... Who...me?...). It is just like the pictures we saw in the John Muir Museum – all the same colours. **Ah reckon John Muir Hud his Heid screwed Oan!"**

Fall in here and you won't be seen again......

"Most of the mountains are ragged and pointed - just the way that you imagine the Rockies and the Sierra Nevada to be. However, seemingly at random, there are also massive grey ones that are completely smooth and rounded, called Domes (I'm sure one of you clever Geologists will be able to tell me why this is) springing up in between. I climbed

halfway up Lambert's Dome and had a peanut butter bagel sitting on a 60 degree slope and moving only..... very....... slowly........."

Peanut butter bagel – hark at me – in the space of a few days I had become an American. I found myself saying things like "Where are the restrooms?", "Do you guys do takeout?" and "Yo Dawg, you is trippin'! Aaa-ight?" (ok I made the last one up but another few days and I would have been saying that....)

Lambert's Dome - just a small example - See me?

Don't move a muscle.... It's not the gradient, the sun bouncing off mah baldy foreheid might cause a snow-melt flash flood......

"The road meanders through the forests and along jaw dropping cliff edges. I Stopped quite a few times, once requiring a few German Bikers to help me get the Harley Back on its feet when I overbalanced whilst stopping. This bike is a monster. It is so heavy that even the slightest overbalance when you are at a standstill and it takes all your might to get it back upright. It is ok when you are moving, the problem is when you stop. I suppose the extra 30 kilos or so that I had stuffed into the panniers and back-box didn't help - another thing to think about when planning....
I am not a small person - 5'10" and a bit.... - but when sitting on it I can JUST reach the kick stand with the tip of my toe. I can also only just reach all the fingertip controls for the radio, cruise control etc when I have my hands on the handgrips. Do they have Giants in Americy? Cos that is who they built this bike for...."

If you happen to have travelled in America - there ARE Giants in rural places. The wife and I got married in rural Montana, on a pure white cliff edge as the snow drifted down, with only the towering fir trees showing through the white mist.

(romantic? who,..... me? - I was just trying to get away on a Snowboard like James Bond at the start of *View to a Kill*. Unfortunately, she caught up with me on her heavily armed Micro-Light Aircraft and decided we were getting hitched right there and then!)

Anyway, whilst there we encountered a lot of real Cowboys – working men who were Rodeo Riders in their spare time. These guys were all 6'6" or more and built like tanks along with it. They would probably ride this Harley in the same way I threw my Honda 600 around when I got home.

....

The next stop I made is right on the road as you follow the Tioga Pass - all you need to do is drive this wonderful road to see the most incredible and "awesome" sights.

"Stopped at an area where you can see right down Yosemite Valley to the overbearing "Half Dome" sticking way up through it. What a sight- it is truly awesome and worth a days' travelling on its own! It is another one of these huge, smooth mountains but this one has been almost completely cut in half. It runs up like a big, smooth ball on one side, reaches the peak, then just goes straight down like a huge axe has chopped it right through the middle.

I ventured to another viewpoint which was signposted to be 200 yards away. It turned out to be 200 yards up a very steep, snow covered hill which was not easy in slick-soled motorbike boots and in about 90 degree heat (strange situation). Imagine Laurel and Hardy in the snow and that was me (you can decide which one I was....) However, it was worth it – a view like that I have never seen.......... It seemed like a hundred miles of grey mountains, green valleys, waterfalls etc. Just wonderful.......

When I returned to the Car Park I was followed around by a largish animal that I had never seen before. It was apparently a Marmot (as a big, tall, gravely-voiced gent told me). He also referred to it as a "Varrmint!!!". I was hallucinating when I saw him produce a giant blunderbus shotgun from his "pants" and blow it away but it wouldn't have been at all strange if he had. However, being followed around by a very tame "Varmint!" added another touch to a fine day."

Looking West with the cut side of "Half Dome" facing you.

Looking back East.

God-damned Varmint!!!

I had another day in Yosemite to come - today was just crossing from one side to the other - but true to form, it still had a surprise even on the way down. You've been up and up, then down, then up then down and down and down. The suddenly you see an almost completely different world - way down below you.....

"Now again you Geologists will be able to tell me why this is..."

(yes I have relations who have the most exciting and action-packed careers in the known world (stress - the KNOWN world - I know a bit about Geology too......)

"I reckon that the general land level on the Western Side of the Sierras is much lower down than on the Eastern Side.
I was coming down the mountains, through the trees and the snowdrifts until I reckoned I had come down as far as I had gone up, and thus should be at the bottom"

I am a Civil Site Engineer- you get a feel for these things after a while.

*. "I was really struggling to negotiate the bike around all the tight hairpin bends, getting **gei** hot (Scottish word) and looking forward to*

being at the bottom. But then I stopped at a viewpoint and there, below, was another 50 miles at least of mountains to descend! However, this was TOTALLY different. Everything up to now had been grey mountains, white snow and green valley lower down. What was ahead was forested, properly forested, and a different colour altogether - a much deeper green with the odd grey tooth of rock sprouting up. It was just like when you see a helicopter's view over the Rainforest on the T.V.. It was like a totally different country – Yosemite has everything……."

Rainforest. This scene is AFTER coming down the other side of the mountains....looking West at what should have been the bottom. There were lakes in the valleys as below. It's no Loch Lomond but no' bad aww the saim.....

But enough of this..... time for something crap! Something that happened to me and can serve as a pitfall to be avoided by you guys. I am so grumpy....

"Then I took a wrong turn.........
There are no bloody signs on rural American roads. You never know where you are heading for, or how many miles away you are from it. You are only sometimes told what the next turning off is going to be and then only on a tiny sign that you often miss. Then when you come to the turning there isn't another sign at it so it's either take pot luck and turn, hoping it's the right one; or carry on and hope that it was only a minor side-road."

This is true. There are very few road signs in rural areas and they aren't big green and white, obvious numbers like we have in Britain. We seem to be in a situation in Britain where if anything bad happens to us, we blame the Government for not making it foolproof (for us fools). "I fell down by not noticing that minor dip in the footpath - the Government should have made it safe enough for me to walk along it without looking where I was going! - sue sue sue!......" As a result, everything has been made completely safe and totally obvious for us, all of the time - hence the giant road signs. Not so elsewhere in the world – in Rural USA, (along with many other Countries) they expect you to look after yourself a bit more which is surprising in the States where litigation is so commonplace.

"There is nowhere to stop – especially on this bike; and you can't just lift up a map as you drive along like you do in a car.
The place is so bloody big that if you do take a wrong turn, as I did, you may then have up to 100 miles to detour – again as I did…….."

Ensen!..... Prepare Grumpy Drive...... Engage!

"The sun was beating down, I was struggling with the bike and I was riding into the sun, full-on for about 2 hours. Ma Coupon Was rrrid-rrraw!"

Translation - "Mah Coupon" - that thing in front of you with a nose, eyes and if you're lucky, two ears. "Rrrid-RRaw"? - just roll your RRRR's like a Scotsman.

"When I finally got to what I thought was Merced (the town I was staying in) – I couldn't find the street I was looking for – very frustrating in 100 degree heat on an overheating 1.7 litre engine. Eventually I went and asked in a dodgy bar in the middle of an Industrial Estate and it turned out I was in the wrong town altogether.....
Had to tackle the freeway for the first time (I knew that full face helmet would come in handy; you can't wear sunglasses in the dark and with the open-face you tend to get eyefuls of bugs at 70mph).
Finally got to Merced at about 9pm. Now this town looked easy to negotiate on multimap.com.... *Spent nearly another 2 hours trying to find my hotel. Merced is quite a sprawling town for this rural area and it doesn't appear to have any structure whatsoever. There are neighbourhoods, then a group of shops, then some more neighbourhoods, then a department store, then more neighbourhoods,*

then an industrial estate with houses in the middle of it and so on and on and on ......

What's more, there is practically no streetlighting. This has the effect of making every neighbourhood look like "the Hood" and is pretty scary for an eedjit like me. Dark roads of wee wooden houses with big, black dudes outside in the middle of the night washing their dodgy motors ....."

Before you jump on my back for racial stereotyping, I am not creating this image and labelling it "The Hood" - rather the media has already done it for me. Every film involving "The Hood" has big, black dudes outside wee white, wooden houses in the middle of the night washing dodgy motors at some stage. Well that was what this was like and conveyed in my under-educated, over-stimulated and let's face it, pin-ball machine mind that I was in "The Hood". Apologies to all.....

"I Was looking for Yosemite Parkway. I found Yosemite Avenue and thought (quite reasonably, no?) that it must be quite near to this. I went all the way along Yosemite Avenue – the problem was it stretched for about 5 miles but had traffic lights every 200 yards!!!!! – aaarrgghh - dark and hot....

Eventually an old drunk told me that Yosemite Parkway was totally the other side of town ........AAAARRRGGGHH!!!"

Captain! The Grumpy-Warp-Drive is overloaded! She canna hold up much longer!

*"Found the hotel just before 11pm - burnt, tired, hungry and thirsty. And when I say Hotel, I mean Motel – not good and run by an Asian couple who were nothing short of rude. However, it was VERY cheap which to a Scotsman is all-forgiving. I walked up to the nearest "restaurant" past more dodgy-looking (in my mind) front garden guys who had an older version of the exact car that the gun-toting Bruce Willis drives in the "Stylo" video. The Restaurant was shut so I walked to the Petrol Station. Whilst there I was accosted by wierdos, then ripped off for **16 dollars** for two tiny hot dogs, 2 bottles of water and 2*

crap beers by an old Daigo (god this is becoming a PC nightmare - I mean a gentleman of Hispanic persuasion – apologies to the many, many people I have offended – I'm going for the record). I scarpered to my room and locked the door....."

Yosmite Proper the Morra.

....

So it all ended well. However, I mentioned *"planning"* once or twice at the beginning of this book. I said that if you didn't plan it properly, your whole trip could be ruined by - and I quote - "fuel shortages; mechanical failures; hotel searching; seeing nothing of interest; and getting ill from too much sun in the desert, too much snow in the mountains, or too much detergent in the cocaine you wake up and find all over you in the drug den you don't remember being taken to.....". Well that night ticked off two of them; and with a bit of bad luck could have ticked off ALL of them (this is The Hood after all......). I planned this trip in detail so the moral of the story here is two-fold:-

- you can never plan enough, and;

- maybe Sat Nav is not such a bad idea after all.......

Thursday - Yosemite Proper

Part 1 - **The Bike**

This is when I finally got to grips with the Electraglide. Any experienced bikers reading this have no doubt been laughing at my complaints up to this point like a Pole Vaulter would look doon on a pathetic wee High-Jumper...... However, taking tight bends on such a heavy bike takes a bit of technique and I only just got it!

The year before this trip, I had been at a small racetrack in Scotland -the mighty Knockhill. You Americans might not have heard of this but I'm sure you've heard of Dario Franchiti - Indy500 Champion. Well, with a name like that you wouldn't imagine that he is a Fifer from Scotland - but he is! and no doubt spent a lot of time racing around this track in his early years as Karting and Formula Vauxhall Junior Champion.

Anyway, I had been given the gift of a track day there - basically you get to do a few laps in a small Racing Car. Beforehand you get a bit of tuition on how to take the bends and so on. Well this suddenly came back to me and saved my hairy ass.....

"Really struggled yesterday. Negotiating these windy mountain roads was just murder. Especially as they have overbanding (crack repairs) all over them and every time your wheel touches one it wants to run along it – giving you a wiggle on the bike.

However, this morning I was thinking about what they taught me at Knockhill – enter corners slow and wide, cut to the inside of the corner as you are going through, accelerate hard then exit fast and wide. Tried this on the bike. What a bloody difference…….. Brake; come in to the bend at the outside of the lane, dropping a gear and revving ready to accelerate; start accelerating through the inside of the lane; then roar out of the corner going wide again – repeat……

This sounds dangerous as you are making the bike lean more but the Harley responded superbly. Up until now I had felt like the Electraglide was in charge, and I was just guiding it along (like Grima Worm-Tongue in Lord of the Rings secretly guiding King Theoden to the will of Saruman……. Geek?... Who..... me?...).
Now I felt fully in control. The bike responded as soon as I started throwing it about a bit. Up to now I had given it too much respect, staying in the middle of the lane and using high gears and low revs.
The bike is a monster. You obviously just have to get it TELT!....."

And do you know, this was such a turning point in my journey that it became the chorus of a song I wrote about the trip...... I am a bit of a Performer (ha ha - "performer"- that doesn't mean I am a good performer!...). This particular song is called **"Heavy Wheels"** and is a minor key, Country-style song. The middle section goes:-

Heavy Wheels on the road
Start out slow and wide......
Gun the engine cutting through
Leave at speed wide and riiiide......

which is basically how the hell you get a Harley Electraglide "aroon" a bend.

You never know, by the time you read this I might have it on the release along with a few others – maybe search the tinterweb for "Mark Curtis - Heavy Wheels" if you are needing to take some punishment for penance.........

  - Part 2 **Yosemite – it just keeps on throwing more and more at you….**

So now I had the bike "Telt", I was free to make my way back into Yosemite for another day. This time I was heading for "Yosemite Village" which was about 80 miles back Eastwards - the way I had come the day before. Now that I had shown the bike who was boss, I actually really enjoyed the long ride in,.
As I entered the mountains again I stopped at a little Gold Prospectors Town called Mariposa. This place was really authentic looking: wooden saloon type buildings; real gold-panning equipment for sale all over the place;... all it needed was a Stage Coach arriving at High Noon and it would be perfect.

I had a quick bite in a most-typical of American Diners - the type you might have seen a waitress roller skating up and down in the fifties....
After that I wandered into a little Gold-Prospectors shop and got

chatting with a huge American who was about the tenth person so far that said "Oh you're from Scaaatland? Hey man..... I'm Scaaadish!"......(not!). He gave me directions to a mad bar I could go to "as you come into L.A." where all the bikers go. The directions were as follows:-

-       Head into Malibu on Pacific Highway 1;
-       Turn left onto "Kenan"
-       Then take a right onto "Mullholland" and it is on your left.

This sounds simple doesn't it? Well it led to a nightmare adventure when I got to L.A. which you can laugh at (at my expense) when you get to chapter 9.

Bridalveil Fall

The road to Bridalveil Fall was the perfect example of Yosemite throwing more and more at you. All the way there I kept stopping to take pictures and video in awe - then I would get ten minutes further on and think "Aw that was a lot of cr*p - *this* is the thing to take pictures of!". Then another ten minutes further on the same would happen again...

"As the road meanders up the mountains, it follows a river - The Merced. I stopped to take pics as it was flowing massively with meltwater and was a cracking sight. However, as always happens, you think summat is good, then a few miles up the road it is better. Sure enough, a few miles on the river became rapids - awesome power. So I stopped to take pics again (prepare to be bored when I return - oh you're bored already?).

However, once again it was upstaged. I came to the Mighty Bridalveil Fall.
Bridalveil Fall is an awesome sight. You park in the very hot car park (I mean temperature-wise - not that the car park was wearing suspenders

and high heels) and then walk up the path that takes you to the foot of the falls. I noticed some people coming the other way were a bit wet - "swimming in the river" I thought........ Aye Right!

The falls are HUGE just now. The sound thunders away and the spray travels for about half a mile in all directions. The path you walk up is under about 4" of flowing water and you are drenched in spray before you get anywhere near the viewpoint.
The water comes down 617 feet and at this time of year, is swollen by meltwater - a sight that just takes your breath away. The sheer power of it, the constant roar and the drenching spray is just.... amazing."

Bridalveil Fall is the most prominent Waterfall in Yosemite Valley. It is so large that, during times of lesser flow, the water doesn't reach the ground at all - turning to mist before it gets there. For this reason, the Ahwahneechee Indians called the Fall "Pohono" which means "Spirit of the Puffing Wind". They also believed that inhaling the spray from the Waterfall increased one's chances of marriage. Well at least I'm safe there then - maybe next time around?......

"Came back down to the car park soaked and feeling cold for the first time since I got off the plane (little did I know - freezing San Francisco loomed but that's a bit later)."

After the mighty falls I didn't expect to see anything as good. But it's true, Yosemite just keeps throwing more and more at you.

"Started up the long mountain road to Glacier Point - a view point that looks down over Yosemite Valley. On the way, just before a tunnel through the mountainside (where I made a lot of noise revving the throaty engine up like a wee eedjit), there is a Vista point that looks back down the valley to the falls. What you don't see when you are down at the falls is that the huge cloud of spray is actually a constant rainbow of refracted light. There's so many different colours it looks like something out of a Fiarytale Land."

(Fairytale Land? - I really think I am becoming Gay as a Vicar's Birthday... aah well, better just embrace it…..)

Actually, the view from this spot really is like a Fairytale Land. The picture came out really well - but no picture could do it justice. Try to imagine a rainbow of colour emerging from the mist at the waterfall.

This picture was zoomed in from about 10 miles away - if you are seeing it in colour, you should just about be able to see Blue, turning to green, to yellow to red in the spray. If you are viewing it in black and white...... - there's a wee bittee coloured spray at the bottom of yon waterfall........

Glacier Point and Half Dome

"Tunnel Viewpoint" was just a quick stop on my way up to Glacier Point. I didn't know much about Glacier Point, apart from that it looked across Yosemite Valley. The road up is quite long, windy and steep...... However, the worst part was the shade. There are long stretches of road that are covered over completely by the fir trees. The combination of altitude and shade made for a bloody cold shorts-clad biker - I revved like a mad-ball and hammered through them as fast as I could, bursting out into the blazing sunshine again with fire emerging from my back tire........ (mmmm, ok....).

"Glacier Point sits at about 7,214 feet (2,199 m). It looks out, straight across Yosemite Valley towards the amazing "Half Dome" on the other side. You can also see Yosemite Falls, Vernal Fall and Nevada Fall. The view is nothing short of spectacular........ It also looks straight down (and I mean straight down!) on Yosemite Valley and Yosemite Village. What a view....."

From this angle you see the true beauty of Half Dome - basically you are at the same height, looking at it full-on from across the valley. It rounds up on one side, full bodied and heavy, then is just shears straight down in the middle like someone took a giant axe to it. It's almost surreal.

And then you look down...... Yosemite Village is straight down, about 3200 feet below. It is bounded on all sides by the rocky slopes of Yosemite Valley which are broken now and again by the spectacular falls.

Just along the path from the viewpoint is a small rock that juts out over the Valley and looks as if it is about to tip over and go crashing down onto Yosemite Village. This rock has a story behind it. In 1872, a "Yosemite Entrepreneur" called James McCauley commissioned the "Four Mile Path" up to Glacier Point. This became a popular place to visit by well-heeled members of society in the early 1900's. It seems, while they were there, they liked to caper about on this rock. When you see it, you will realise that this was a rather precarious (nay suicidal) way to carry on. There are even indications that people were married on it! No way to run from the alter in that case (unless suicide is the only other option to marriage....... a common lament).

You can just make out the mighty Yosemite Falls to the right.

Here is the rock in question. It is imaginatively named......... wait forrrrrr it...........

Overhanging Rock!

Now just the fact that it doesn't seem to be attached to the rest of the rocks would be enough to put me off, but not those Crazy, early 1900's, thrill-seekers.

If you have a search on the Tinterweb you can see a photo of Kitty Tatch and Katherine Hazelston, dancing on the end of this rock in 1900. It is a sign of how popular the area had already become that they were both Waitresses at Hotels in the park.

These days the Health and Safety Laws are a little more stringent and there is a fence up.

"The Government should have stopped me from going to the end of that precarious rock and nearly falling off! How can I be expected to know that it is dangerous - there are No SIGNS! Sue! Sue! Sue!...."

As I might have mentioned, I am a Jags Fan - the Mighty Partick Thistle Football Club of Glasgow. Now we get around three thousand or more of a crowd most weeks - considerably dwarfed by the other two teams in Glasgow (Rangers and Celtic......you might have heard of these small outfits) who can get almost 60,000. But do they have pictures of their fans in locations like THIS!!!

Aye right!

"Coming back from Yosemite tonight, it suddenly got really cold and I was in shorts, t-shirt and trainers. Chased the sun Westwards (like my son Kieran chasing after the Ice Cream Van) as it went down all the way back to try to warm up and really put the bike through its paces – Awesome!!! (Sorry, I'm from Americy now)…!"

It is about 100 miles from Glacier Point down the mountains and out to Merced and it turned cold..... You know the old story about punishment in Purgatory where the person is massively hungry but can never quite reach the bunch of grapes hanging in front of them? Well this was like that (Aye it was just as bad, right!....). The sun was peeking over the mountains ahead, just too high for its warming rays to hit me; so I would hammer down, past the peaks, only to find it had gone down a touch more and was now beyond the next set of peaks...... and so on.... The problem is, the faster you go on a bike, the colder you get. Maybe, just maybe, it would have been wiser to stop and get the cold weather bike gear out instead of just chasing the sun in shorts and t-shirt....... However was fun roaring through the little villages and wide, lonely prairies........

"Got back too late for food again. This time took the bike around a few streets and found a couple of bars blaring out rap music blended with lots of shouting. As usual, these looked daunting due to all American films portraying everywhere playing rap and hip hop as dangerous. So of course, I went in...., and found, as expected, that they are all just normal blokes having a good time - they just express it by shouting a lot.

Sat down next to a guy who announced that he was "Scaddish too!". AAAArrrgghhhh!

"I was about to set this latest Usurper straight but then he went on to tell me his parents were from Ayrshire."

Awwwright, Ah'll gie yoo that wan....

"What's more he had spent the last 3 years travelling the states playing guitar - cue interesting conversations with lots of "Dude"s thrown in. He is sending me some of his material...

Left there about midnight - thank God for Dinnys"

You see, there's that name again..... As a footnote to the evening, here is one of my latest and greatest achievements of common sense and organisation.

"I had washed all my clothes (and pretty much flooded the place) before leaving for Yosemite this morning. I then left the Air Conditioning on full blast all day and returned tonight to a freezing cold, damp room full of wet clothes....."

In my defence, I am from Scotland where Air Conditioning is just a fictional process that they use to help sell cars - "Whit's that Air-coan button there - some soart o' fancy heater like?"

"San Francisco the Morra!"

Final word.

The next morning opened my eyes to something that I always knew was there, but hadn't really thought about that much.

"Chinese for breakfast - god I love this place........"

(ha ha, no, not that.....)

"Bought some supplies from a Mexican Supermarket then had a look in the Gun Store next door - a huge array of killing devices. They had a firing range and I thought I might go in and shoot a couple of handguns like Mel Gibson (I know I'm better looking but I am prepared to downgrade a bit for the craic). However, I was put off by the conversation that an old-ish, tall, skinny, bearded, heavy metal t-shirted man was having with the shop assistant. He was looking at dum dum bullets - hollow points.

The shop assistant was proudly going on about what happens when they hit the body – "what these do is just open out when they enter whatever they hit and create a huge mess". I assumed he was talking about Deer as most of the shop was for hunting.
However, then the bearded fella said "Yeah man I think I'll go for the hollow points - If I shoot somebody I don't want them getting up again......."

I got out of there sharpish."

I'm all for a bit of mindless violence between friends, but let's keep a lid on it eh?
(a political statement by Mark Curtis)

Chapter 5- San Francisco

The Historic Blues, the Histrionic Booze and some rather unusual Chaps…..

There are several points I need to cover about the trip to San Francisco. They are as follows:-

 1. The Freeway - Jesus! I Really don't think there are any rules (and I hadn't even got to LA yet....)

 2. The Cold - Whit's going on? From Merced to San Francisco the temp went from Barbados, to Banff (this could be either of: the mountain, ski resort in Alberta, Canada; or equally the wee village on the North East Coast of Scotland next to the excellently named...... MacDuff!)

 3. The Hills and Tramlines - Steve McQueen, Clint Eastwood, and then ME..

 4. The Locals - Cosmopolitan and Slim! - Are these people from Europe?

 5. The Bars, The Blues and The Gay Parades (no comment)

I experienced pretty much all of these in one day……

Day 1 – All of the Above

San Francisco is on a Peninsula - The San Francisco Peninsula to be precise - and is bounded on three sides by water. Aside from the protected city parks, the City covers *every inch* of this peninsula; and with over 800,000 people, it is apparently the 2nd most densely populated city in North America.

The Peninsula (and hence the City on top of it) is formed of a series of steep hills. Many of these hills have been named and will sound familiar such as "Pacific Heights", "Twin Peaks" and so on (a thought entered my head that this one might've been better named "Top Heavy Luvlies). As with most American Cities they have tried to build a lot of the city on a grid system. However, this is not easy on a series of steep hills and it makes for some strange street layouts. Often, as you descend a steep hill on one street, it is crossed transversely by other streets, which run along the side of the hill. Since the transverse ones are level, it has the effect of the making the downhill street suddenly stop going steeply downhill and go level for a few metres at each intersexual (sorry, I have never been able to call an Intersection anything else since I got to the US) before suddenly diving down again. This is best-shown by the famous car chase in the 1968 Steve McQueen classic - "*Bullitt*".

If you have never seen this film, I will be amazed if you haven't seen the famous car chase through San Francisco. A green, 1968 Ford Mustang GT Fastback chasing a V8 Dodge Charger with both basically hammering down the steep hills, bottoming out when they hit each level, transverse road, then jumping off it to carry on down the hill........ classic! I attempted this later…..

San Francisco can be reached from the South by driving up the Peninsula. However, other than that you have to cross the San Francisco Bay either on the Bay Bridge running from the East mainland; or the Golden Gate Bridge running from the Marin Headlands to the North.

My journey from Merced would take me straight up "Golden State Highway 99" North-West as far as Manteca - then a series of Freeways straight-West until I came to the San Francisco Bay Area. From there I would turn North to Oakland and cross the Bay Bridge to San Francisco - about 130 miles all-in-all.

The journey was not fun.... Being used to the proper and correct 3-lanes-per-direction on the British Motorways, you would think I would be in heaven drifting across the massively wide, concrete runways that the Americans have linking every town and city with..... not so.

There is actually a serious point to make here. If you are going to try a bike tour in the States and have not experienced the Freeways before, it is a good idea to take a test run when the freeways are quiet - just to get the feel for it. I didn't do this, but luckily I did have a reasonably gentle introduction to the freeway by joining at Merced - out in the countryside having had several days to get used to the bike on more rural routes. I then progressed to larger and busier Highways and Freeways as the journey went on. You will see from the following that I was still pretty shocked. Later in the book you will also hear of my experience trying to get into Central L.A. which was more than a little terrifying.

The point being that if I had got off of a plane in L.A. as a novice Harley Free Spirit, hired a bike, then gone straight out onto the crazy L.A. Freeways; I would have had such a shock that I probably would have abandoned the bike and taken the train from there on...... give yourself a chance to get the hang of it........

So it began....

*"Freeway for a hundred miles or so to San Fran. NOT fun. The roads range from 6 lanes to **10 lanes** wide (3 to 5 lanes on each side). However, they bloody need that - there doesn't seem to be any structure at all like the slow traffic going on the outside and the fast traffic on the inside - they just zoom up any lane - all the time."*

I continued.

*"I am not even sure if there **IS** a rule about which lane to use. Also the roads are concrete with overbanded cracks everywhere - NOT good when you are on two wheels."*

The non-biker will never understand the effect those little lines of poured-out bitumen to cover the cracks, have on a bike. Your wheel decides, just for an instant, that it wants to run along the line of the overbanding, rather than the direction you are telling it to go. Just for that instant you get a rather terrifying wobble and sensation of losing control which it takes a while to get used to. However, on this particular route, once you do get used to it, you are in for a further shock when you get to San Francisco - multiply that momentary wobble by 100 and that is the sensation of trying to cross a San Francisco Tramline which is running alongside you.......

"3 hours of extreme concentration. Drank 2 litres of water out of my rucksack en-route."

So I made it there unscathed but it was an eye-opener. I imagine I was probably sitting bolt upright and tense, like an American Cop - the total opposite of the other Harley Riders I noticed on the way. They would pass in the sort of Easy Rider getup, with one hand dangling down almost touching the road as they lay back on their customised bikes. In fact they were so casual that their entire bodies seemed to droop down in a fashion that said "I ain't gonna take any sh#t from THE MAN" as if they were just hanging off of those high-up, chopper handlebars....

Now here's another piece of info for the prospective Tourer.

"Thank God for Google Earth."

(Other God-like satellite-based planet-viewers are available....., probably)

"I didn't think I would be able to find my hotel; so before I left, I took myself along the whole route to it from the Bay Bridge using "Streetview". This took a while in the hotel room but it was worth it. When I got to San Fran I already knew the look of the turnpike when I approached it; the crossings; the streets and so on and found the hotel nae bodgers....

It was cracking to go over the Bay Bridge and see Alcatraz and the Golden Gate Bridge away on the distance."

This is a spectacular way to get into San Francisco. Everyone has heard of the Golden Gate Bridge (which you would cross to get to San Francisco from the North). It does look impressive from the outside, but, when you cross it, you canny see anything as the sides are too high! It's a big let-down. The Bay Bridge however, is much longer and you can see everything - especially if you are going West (into San Francisco) as you are on the top deck.

Bay Bridge is pretty impressive itself - it has two spans of approximately 3100m each. These are broken in the middle by Yerba Buena Island, on which you find yourself running through a tunnel between the bridge spans - a bit strange. Both spans have a bottom deck for traffic going East (out of San Francisco) and a top deck for the Westies. The top deck is fantastic.

Initially the theme tune to "Taxi" runs through your head as you recognise you are pretty much in the starting credits to the show - you know the one - doo doo doo doo doo doo doo-ooo doo doo doo doo doo doo doo-ooo doo doooooo...... DarNar! DarNar! Doop! (any more explanation needed than that, I don't think so) but you soon catch site of *Treasure Island* to your right. This is actually a man-made island of an almost perfect octagonal shape. It sits just off of Yerba Buena Island which splits the two bridge spans. It was built for the San Francisco World's Fair of 1939. Interestingly it was also designated for use as an Airport for Pan American World Airways Flying Boats! Images of Indiana Jones or maybe Cary Grant in his exotic pilot garb spring to mind. However, you soon forget that when you see the Mighty *Alcatraz* in the distance. We'll get to that........

First, Parking....

*"Parking! AAArrgh. The Hotel doesn't have parking and they said the cheapest parking garage was 32 dollars per night and 20 dollars **per hour** during the day. I went over and checked this and they also said that if I took the bike out for a spin in the evening I would have to pay the whole thing AGAIN on my return."*

However, here is one of the first of many quirky, inspired and downright excellent things I encountered in San Francisco.

"I had read in Lonely Planet that SF is a bike friendly city. I consulted it again for details and sure enough there are loads of tiny spaces for motor-bikes - all over the City. These face out the way from the kerb and have their own meters at about a tenth of the price for cars. Why can't WE do this? I can only think of two places in Glasgow City Centre that are just for bike parking and they have about 10 spaces each - always full..... How simple is this!"

Once parked and moved-in, I took the bike back out for a look around. Initially I went along the coast, up to and through the Fisherman's Wharf area. This takes you past all the Piers originally used for trade. The Piers are numbered, with "*Pier 39*" perhaps being the most famous which adorns many a souvenir baseball cap. "*Fishermans Wharf*" just further along is the touristy area with views over to Alcatraz and a whole plethora of boat trips available (including a giant "Rocket Boat" which looked rather interesting).

"I pulled up at a car park at Fisherman's Wharf and there were at least a hundred bikers there. Felt quite at home and very virile and masculine in-about all the other petrol-heids.
Then, suddenly, they all left at once in a huge, roaring procession.
Cool.

However, to go from one extreme to the other, within 5 minutes, there came a massive procession of Gay Cyclists through the same street. Honestly there were at least a thousand of them and they had pink banners and had YMCA-esque music hammering out of big, pink speakers they were towing on special bike-pulled carts..
Just remembered - this is gay pride weekend...... San Francisco is one quirky city."

And no, I didn't book this entire trip to enable me to be in San Francisco on these exact two days........

Ok I did. Men for pleasure - Women for Babies!

(actually no I didn't.... apologies for the nth offensive remark....)

"Crossed the Golden Gate at Sunset"

Well that sounds kind of romantic doesn't it; crossing the Golden Gate Bridge at sunset...... It certainly looked beautiful on the way along the coast with the sun shining through it.

I took this from the saddle of the Harley - canny beat it.......

Get on the bridge though, and you find that the road is at a lower level than the footpaths at either side. Unless you are driving a truck, all you see is grey tar, red super-structure, and sky.
(Bubble..... pin....... bang!)
Also, there was another slight problem with it that we will come to in a minute.

"Went down to the expensive area at the other side and cruised about..."

As you exit the Golden Gate Bridge you enter the Marin Headlands. This is the southernmost tip of Marin County and is a hilly area which commands some fabulous views over the bay. The Coastal area to the East of this is called Sausalito. This was a thriving ship building area during World War Two but has now morphed into a rather up-market community. This is pretty apparent when you spot some of the large, glass fronted houses perched on the hillside looking over the "'Frisco Bay"....

However, in amongst Sausalito is a large community of Houseboat Dwellers (or as they prefer to call them - "Floating Homes"). These are a wonderful mixture of higgledy-piggledy shapes and colours as you can see. You might think of this as a community of travelling, free-spirits bringing the repute of the area down for the well-heeled Land-Dwellers..... Not so. A quick look on the tinterweb sees these "Floating Homes" as selling for between $300,000 and $1,000,000!

On the way back across I began to realise I wasn't in the desert any more. San Francisco is surprisingly cold - in fact it is:-

"Absolutely Bloody FREEZING. Have hardly worn the bike jacket at all up to now - had it on tonight along with the big gloves and full face helmet and by the time I got back I was frozen - fingers were numb for hours."

You just can't assume anything on a trip like this - I never imagined it would feel colder in San Francisco than it did on top of the Sierra Nevada Mountains........ But it certainly did.

Then the mental roads reared their ugly head again.....

"Crossing the bridge southwards was nothing short of crazy. They drive like lunatics here. After coming off the bridge on the South side there was an area where construction work suddenly merged 5 lanes into 2 lanes. This wasn't like in Britain, with loads of signs, flashing orange lights and white lines giving you lots of warning and guiding you gently

across - oh no....... This was just everybody doing 70mph, trying to suddenly cut across into other lanes without slowing down, all at the exact instant the cones appeared in front of them in their own lane. Had to put the bike through its paces to get out of trouble several times."

In my head this is like the scene in *The Matrix Reloaded* when the bold *Trinity* is hammering up the freeway in the wrong direction, weaving in and out frantically on a big Ducati........ In reality, it was probably mundane as a tired fruit bowl. However, the Electraglide is not the most manoeuvrable of bikes and a lot of quick reactions and roaring thrusts into spaces was required...... Again – if possible, try to get used to the City Roads in the US before taking your bike out.

So, anyway, on to Steve McQueen.......

Everyone remembers *that* scene from *Bullitt* which I mentioned earlier. Well I thought I would do the same thing - head up to the top of one of the hills then hammer down it, roaring off of each transverse road crossing my path, with the wheels thudding down onto the next downhill.

So, I did it............ very slowly....... It turns out there are traffic lights at pretty much every intersexual which means: slow-down; stop; traverse the level area; speed up again. Great..... Actually, it *was* pretty damn exciting but for all the wrong reasons.

" I reckon this bike is too big for a city like this. Stopping at each intersexual on a steep slope is not easy. Also, the roads are in a state, half of the streets are one way and I was constantly thinking I was going the wrong way down them. The worst though are the tram lines. These are everywhere and take your wheels along them in a way the overbanding on the freeway could only aspire to - they really could throw you off. You have to stay at one side (there isn't much room) then really commit to crossing them to get into the middle, then do the same again."

Beginning to think Ensen has engaged the Grumpy Warp Drive again? Probably right.

"Struggled to find the hotel and was frozen solid when I parked up...... Not moving the bike again until Sunday - parking tickets or not."

Good start eh? That was the hills, the cold and the mad driving experienced. Not been too impressed with San Francisco yet? At this point I felt the same - after the wonders of Yosemite it just didn't have the same wow factor. However, soon I started to enjoy San Francisco for different reasons - the nights out and the Blues Bar for starters!

"Later, I had about the best burger meal I have ever had in the hotel pub - I didn't think you could actually do anything with a burger to make it different but they know what they are doing here...... Ridiculous really as the bar was modelled on an "English Pub" but the beef/horse burger and measly portion of chunky chips you would get in Britain couldn't even begin to compare.

After taking a bit of advice from the Barmaid (THL)...... I went up to "Broadway" which is apparently the Italian Quarter and the place to be. What surprised me was that the first place I saw was a strip club,..... and the 2nd..... However, I soon realised that this is a place along the lines of Soho in London where there are some of the seediest places in the City, right next door to some of the most respected clubs and restaurants. It was really quirky too – some very unusual bars and restaurants based on a huge array of nationalities. This city is so much more cosmopolitan than everywhere else I have been since I got to the States. "

I think "quirky" is a really good word to describe San Francisco. You would describe it thus in the same way you might describe somewhere like Notting Hill or Camden in London as quirky – filled with a huge array of different types of people all bringing their own special traits and customs to the area. The people mostly seemed quite quiet and well educated, and were dressed differently; often in the sort of understated, sometimes quirky way you see in university towns in England. Walking around San Francisco in the daytime, I felt I could have been in a European City.

Of course, now and again you see the most flamboyant and outrageous, roller-skating, pink haired, glittering bumble-bee types but in San Fancisco this doesn't cause a 2nd glance....

An example of the posh but quirky restaurants lining the streets.

But the fun was about to start.....
"Went into a sports bar and got pinned in the corner as two guys had a fight over a game of pool - cracking."

It's quite fun to see a bar fight in the States. For one thing, a lot of the blokes are just huge. But secondly, sometimes it seems that as big a part as the actual violence, is who can make the best and most cutting put-down or threat to the other guy. Looking cool in the States is very important....

This particular fight was between a couple if big lads. One was strong and silent and looked pretty dangerous. The other was also huge but was a total mouthpiece. After a massive one-way stream of insults and put downs, they started throwing a few haymakers and managed to burl themselves my way. I set my shoulders to *stun* in the way I coach my kid's football team to do to fend off tackles and bounced them back into the ring a few times.......... Eventually they cooled down and just started the game again…. Nice. However, the best was still to come as I left.

"As I was wandering along the street, I overheard a conversation and as a result managed to find the only blues bar in the area - possibly in the whole city. I went in and there were a few old guys playing. Sounded pretty average at first - then they got warmed up... They were bloody superb.

I sat at the end of the bar with a guy called Rik (or RRRRiccckkkk as he put it) who looked exactly like one of the ZZ Top guys; drinking shots of Jim Beam and happy as Mr Happy from Happington..... (who just won first prize in the happy competition).
Rrrriccckkkkk went on and on about an old blues band called the "Almond Brothers". I even asked him to spell this – definitely ***Almond****....????"*

As you may have guessed a certain amount of alcohol had been consumed by this point and the bold Rik actually meant the 1970's Blues Rock outfit The Allman Brothers Band.
Rik loved this crew and I can only hope he hasn't really spent the last 40 years referring to them as a pair of blood-related, sweet nuts………

"Even the barmaid was just so San Francisco - about 70 years old, wearing a low-cut black, mini dress; black hair all back combed and

massive; eyeliner like black lightening and smiling, laughing, dancing and working constantly....... This is real, classic San-Francisco.

Left at 2am with a Happy-Heid and as a result, I am still in my hotel room at 1pm the next "morning" catching up on correspondence........ Was totally worth it though."

What I had stumbled across was **"The Saloon"** which claims to be the oldest bar in San Francisco. It is said to have survived the Great San Francisco Earthquake of 1906 due to its "unusually stout" timbers. However, it is also said to have survived the fires that raged through the city for several days after. This was apparently due to the men of the Fire Department having a strong tendency to protect the ladies of ill repute who lived upstairs.......
Sounds about right for a growly, corner blues bar.

"The place is really small and basic - a real blues bar. No fancy sound system, a couple of big old amps on the "stage" and a couple of ancient spotlights shining down, and that's it!"

It is actually the most authentic blues bar I have ever seen (though whether this is by design, or whether it has just remained the way it is for countless years due to no-one having the thought of upgrading it - I cannot say).
It has a very unassuming frontage - the kind of bar that you might see up some of the less salubrious side streets in Glasgow which most folk wouldn't go in unless they knew someone..... It has a lot of unvarnished wood; the stage is just a raised wooden area lit by hanging light bulbs and with some old, stack amps piled up at the back. It is deliciously raw and the growling tones of the bands that night, just fit right in.
It is well respected too and some well-known names play there regularly. Ron Hacker who played the second night I was there, is pretty highly regarded in the Blues circles. Inside the cover of the CD I bought while there, the biographer mentions that someone once asked Ron why he never plays any Stevie Ray Vaughan songs. He replied

"because me and Stevie made a pact - never to play each other's songs.......". And they never have.

I just loved this place. Blues, alcohol, and a dive bar is how I imagine heaven. Me and Rrriickkkk had a rare time at the end of the bar....... "The Saloon" can be found at 1232 Grant, San Francisco, CA94133; and is WELL worth a visit if you ever hit the San Fran.......

Ron Hacker. Check out the peeling wallpaper and fantastic stage background. Love it!

The unassuming frontage of a great bar.

So by the end of the first night I had experienced The Freeway; the Cold; The Hills and Tramlines; the Locals; the Bars; the Blues and the Gay Parades….. Not bad for one day. So for day two the bike was ditched and I went for a walk………

Day 2 – The Walk

So off I went, walking all the way past all the old trade piers towards Fishermans' Wharf. At first, this was not what I had hoped for as my email home the day after began to tell.

"Well I got a bit bored for the first time yesterday. Walked all the way to the Fisherman's Wharf area. Now it is totally awesome to look out and see the Golden Gate Bridge, Alcatraz and all the sailing boats. However, once you have done that and sampled the seafood, all that is left is miles of tourist shops. I toured these for prezzies to bring home and bought nothing so you can all suffer….."

Don't be put off by this ridiculous paragraph. I qualified it slightly afterwards....

"Of course, there are LOADS of interesting things to see and do in a city like SF but I have been spoiled for the last two weeks by awesomeness being thrown at me all of the time (by Yosemite). Not used to having to go and look for it!"

The walk up past all the old trade piers is actually quite interesting. There are still reminders of a fading age such as the odd, giant-fruit market and working boat yard. There are also new takes on a trade pier such as this intriguing place.

(Homer Simpson Voice)   Mmmmm.... Choc-litt.......

The further North you go, the closer you get to all of the touristy places and you also begin to see the mighty Alcatraz across the water. Alcatraz is really impressive - a High Security Jail out in the middle of the city bay. The only place I have seen similar to this is Fort Boyard in France though this has a different history.

As you get towards Fishermans Wharf you start to get the tourist traps. There is an amazing array of boats with trips being offered; loads of street performers and so on. When you reach the famous "Pier 39" you hit the real tourist spot. This just consists of a huge boardwalk of shops and yes, I looked all over it and bought nothing.

A note to anyone planning a visit to San Francisco. The Alcatraz tours are apparently very good - especially the night visits...... spooOOOKYYyyy. However, if you want to do one, book well in advance! I missed out on this as was booked solid all weekend.

Boats old and new in the bay.

The wonderfully menacing....... ALCATRAZ!

Check this mother, dredging the bay.

Rocket Boat - fancy a punt dear?

"My plan had been to leave the bike and get some exercise by walking many miles. However, having done that, I skilfully counteracted it by having fried seafood for lunch...."

No-one can say I'm not balanced..... Actually the seafood in Fisherman's wharf is well renowned, especially the clam chowder, so I wanted a go.....

"Desiring a proper sample, I splashed out and ordered the chef's platter. Little did I know that the huge array of Aquatic Life would be surrounded in the thickest, heaviest, greasiest batter I have ever seen......

and it came with chips!"

Even as someone who comes from the home of the deep-fried Mars Bar, I still thought the batter totally ruined some good fish. However, the clam chowder was VERY good! Is it just me, or does Clam Chowder sound like something a dog would order in Starbarks?

Before leaving the "Wharf" I was accosted by very large, obviously quite deranged chap who came up and called me a "c##k-sucker" and then gave me the kind of look that Fred - the homeless guy in Back to the Future - gives to Marti McFly when he finally bursts back into 1985....... (another fine literary reference... What is wrong with me? I have a degree you know.......)
I had to wonder what it was about me that made him weave through the crowds of other (and in my opinion much more worthy of insulting) people to specifically insult me........
Maybe I'm just lucky.

So, these minor events had me feeling mildly amused (Yosemite. You have a lot to answer for!). However, things just got better throughout the day, as they always seem to do on this trip...

"I then walked inland, up over one of the steep, Steve McQueen hills. It seems a very strange place to build a city: at sea-level all around the outside; but on a series of VERY steep and pointed hills in the middle.

Anyway, it was a nice walk and I needed to go to a chemist for a massive sore I had on my lip from motorcycling through hot weather with no face-shield. The walk ended in some awesomeness."

Before the "awesomeness" another word of advice for potential bikers in this country. As it is (mainly) rather warm in the summer, you tend to use an open-faced helmet. Take some sort of Lip Salve! Your face dries out from the wind, then you start to get cold sores all over your lips. I remarked to my wife on the phone that no women would want to come near me in San Francisco due to the open-sores and the twitching from the agony whenever I smiled and it cracked the dried skin.......... It's hard to be charming without smiling......

"Coming out of the Chemist I noted that USA were playing Mexico in the final of the Gold Cup - "that'll do me!". Found a Sports bar and watched it with the USA crowd - and when I say the USA crowd, I mean the "USA!... USA!...USA!..." crowd as that is apparently the only song they know....
Actually, I had a really good time. Some of them were a bit clueless on the football front (why would they know much about soccer in a place where "football" means something different altogether) but I was talking to one young guy whose "Soccer" knowledge about the premiership and the Spanish leagues was probably better than mine. He knew all the rules and tactics too - unusual for an American! However, he ruined it when discussing Everton, remarking that they were from London. People get shot in Liverpool for lesser insolence!.... Ooooh . So close!

By the time I had sunk a few beers watching this (USA lost 4 -2 by the way), it was nearly 8pm - out for the night then!

*I discovered I was on "Broadway" but on the other side of the hill, so I walked right up and over it again - this was really nice as it was dusk. It's great to be able to walk around American cities. Once you know what areas **not** to go to, you can go wherever else you want. I have been told several times that I will know right away if I go into the* *wrong area, and to just to turn around. I assumed it would be all chain link fences and rap music....... (cultural stereotyping again.....) But in these parts, they are all to the south of the Market area which I am not anywhere near."*

I took one or two pictures as I was making my way of the hill - to get a sense of just how steep they really are.......

It just feels strange as you hike up and down.

Oh come on!

"Sadly, I noticed that there were a lot of homeless on the streets of San Fran. I suppose such a free and cosmopolitan town is an attractive place when you are down on your luck. They didn't tend to bother anyone from what I saw but they did, however, bother each other - I watched one creep up on another who was asleep and give him a huge kick - the other jumped up and chased him away with the most cleverly all-encompassing, racists curse I have ever heard:-

"F**king Chinese Nigger!"......

Anyway, I managed to find the blues bar again.
Tonight there was an old Blues Guitarist on called Ron Hacker. He is quite famous but shy's away from any fame. Then guess what - I met a couple of blokes from Dundee! - Everywhere I go I am running into Scots doing a tour like I am. For the first hour, I was absolutely convinced that they were here for Gay Pride - both were wearing casual shirts but buttoned up to the neck; one of them had a sort of Gerard Kelly look going on with the black, waved hair and black leather jacket; and they looked a bit sheepish when I asked them what they were doing here.

However, after some very careful conversations, I discovered that they weren't.....
When I told them what I had thought, - they said that loads of people think that they are..... ha ha"

No smoke without fire boys!...... x

"The old Queen of San Francisco (as I now think of her) was behind the bar again. I tried to get some video of her this time. I have revised my age assessment - I reckon she is more like 80 than 70. Frail, a little stooped. However, once again in a low-cut top and mini skirt with black eyeliner and dancing and smiling and pouring drinks non-stop for hour upon hour upon hour. The bloke behind the bar is a huge, classic "American Man" who looks like an ex-marine. He is called Oggy.....and

tonight seemed to be aggressively serving completely random drinks, no matter what was requested by the punters.....

"You'll drink it or you can F##k Off!!!"

Well I stayed in the bar until the band finished again at about 2am - drinking Jim Beam like a professional. Then, in the words of the song (probably) "A slice of pizza then bed" - god I love this place......."

And, that was the end of my visit to this quirkiest of Cities. I enjoyed the Frisco and, as with so many places I visited on this tour, I left a piece of my heart there. This is rather like the Angel that went to the birthday party of his mate "San-Fran" down in Hell. It was a bit of a disco and rather raucous. The Angel had a tad too much to drink and forgot his harp. The next day he had to go and see the big yin where he said "Really sorry God, but I left my harp in San-Fran's Disco".

However, tomorrow was another day and a ride leading to what I expected to be the coolest place on my trip – Santa Cruz..........

Chapter 6 - Santa Cruz

Quaint Seaside Village.......

Santa Cruz....... The name conjures up images of Hippies; Skateboarders with trousers hanging down to show imitation pants; seaside boardwalks and, if you are of a certain age; vampires riding around on motorbikes, enticing permed-haired, teenagers to join their evil gang........

I didn't find it quite that way.

First Some History

The town of Santa Cruz, meaning "Holy Cross" was, like so many American towns, initiated by Spanish Colonialists. Prior to this there were various settlements of Ohlone Indians around the area, but in 1791, Father Fermin Lasuen founded *La Misión de la Exaltación de la Santa Cruz -* or Mission Santa Cruz - to convert the surrounding Ohlone settlements to Catholicism. This was the start of the Santa Cruz we know today.

....

I feel this an appropriate point to add in some more general history – something which had a massive effect on the shaping of not only this area's future; but also of all other areas visited in this book.

Everywhere we have been so far, was at one time the territory of Mexico. The change which led to the shaping of the states we know today was sparked by a place we all know as (All my Ex's live in....) Texas.

In 1821 Mexico finally declared itself independent from Spanish rule after 11 years of guerrilla war. At this time, Mexico not only had control of the Santa Cruz area; it encompassed all of the states we know today as Texas, New Mexico, Arizona, Utah, Nevada, California and parts of Wyoming and Colorado.

The big change was sparked off in Texas. Throughout the 1820s there was a large migration of US Citizens into Texas which led to the Mexican Government raising property taxes, raising taxes on imported American goods and even abolishing slavery (outrageous!....). The Texans didn't like that and a long struggle ensued.
As the American influx continued, the conflict increased until, in 1835, the Texan Army, supported by volunteers from America, chased the Mexican Military out of Texas. Soon after, in 1836, Texas declared itself an Independent Republic and appointed new leadership. Unsurprisingly Mexico refused to recognise this and the conflict escalated and carried on into the 1840's.

Eventually, on 29th December 1845, James Knox Polk – President of the United States of America, signed a Bill accepting Texas as the 28th State of the Union. In effect, the USA "annexed off" Texas (where have we heard that phrase in recent history?....). This was the spark that started the Mexican American War of 1845 to 1848.

During the next two years, the American Army managed to drive the Mexican Military out of the states we know today as California, Nevada, Arizona, Utah, New Mexico, Wyoming, Colorado and of course, Texas. The treaty of Guadalupe Hildago was signed on 2nd February 1848, gifting the Mexican Government around $15 million and offering Mexican Citizens living in these areas the opportunity to either leave, or become Citizens of the USA (which almost all of them did). The Southern Texan border was agreed as the Rio Grande River which is how it still stands today.

....

Back to Santa Cruz. In contrast to its modern reputation for Liberalism and Anti-War Activism; Santa Cruz had a sizeable Gunpowder Industry going on throughout the late 1900's. The California Powder Works became a large producer of Gunpowder after the American Civil War cut off supplies to the Mining and Road Building Industries. It carried on creating Gunpowder for these Industries, and the military, until it finally closed its doors in 1914.

These days Santa Cruz is known for: Liberalism (it was one of the first American Cities to approve the medical use of Marijuana); Social Activism (the first City Council in the U.S. to denounce the Iraq war); Rehabilitation (a well-known Council-sponsored community program for rehabilitating Military Veterans back into Society) and of course beach-based fun (the Santa Cruz Beach Boardwalk has been operating continuously since 1907!). With a sizeable Campus of the University of California there too, it has a bit of everything.

The Journey to Santa Cruz

So I left San Francisco on a beautiful, sunny morning, a bit sad and with a rather "sair heid". Typically for the 'Frisco it was cold and sharp along with the sunshine and the full-face helmet was on again. I made my way West, out of the main city, intending on getting to the coast then heading South. This really isn't too bad once you get out of the tourist and business areas. After running through the outskirts, I suddenly found myself on the West Coast and stopped at a wonderful golf course. It was lush and green and looked out over the Golden Gate Bridge but looking from the West side this time. What a view.....

Everything seeeds a little more tranquil on this side of the bridge. I imagined what it would be like to Tee-Off down the beautiful, quiet, lush, green fairway with the Golden Gate Bridge taunting you with its magnificence from the front-left. This wouldn't help my game at all! The bridge would almost certainly be the latest addition to my list of naturally ball-magnetic items; just like clumps of trees, large rocks, cars!!!! and any other physical impedances.

Interestingly, there were little three wheeled things that looked like sporty golf carts going by all the time,...... but on the main road. These turned out to be Guided-Tour-Cars. They don't quite drive themselves but have a wee sat-nav which tells you the route you should take around the city and blasts you with information as you pass all the landmarks along the way. Americans really know how to make money from innovations...... You would imagine little gimmicks like a 3-wheeled touring buggy would be just for skimming around the town centre but no, these ones ventured well out into the styx…..

Now for a cracking ride down the coast I thought........ Well that didn't happen. It seemed to me at the time (in my usual erroneous and stereotypical manner) that a large number of Americans aren't too used to driving on roads that aren't several lanes wide.

"I think it must be the beginning of the holidays here. The coast road was jammed solid and it doesn't seem to be the done thing to jump the queue on a bike the way we do in Britain. Very slow journey.

After a couple of hours of pointless queuing on a single carriageway I came to the cause - one o' those crazy, new-fangled...... JUNCTIONS. Yes that was it..... a junction. Jesus guys, learn to filter. I pulled in to a wee gravel car park for a break and met a couple of young lads on sport bikes. Sure enough, they said that it's illegal there to run up between the traffic on a bike and added the wonderfully descriptive comment "There's usually some PUNK-ASS Cop at the end". Well that was me telt!"

I suppose the serious point here is that it is illegal to run up the outside of traffic queues on a bike in California. However, I would be tempted to try playing the dumb tourist at least a couple of times…..

Basically, I was headed for **Pacific Highway 1**. If you ever take a tour on the West Coast, you should definitely take a run down this road! What we know today as Pacific Highway 1 is really called "State Route 1". It began as a collection of shorter stretches of road, running along the coastline. These were eventually collectivised and re-named (in the 1964 State Highway Renumbering if you want to be exact) as "State Route 1"

State Route 1 runs from a tiny village called Legget, about 180 miles north of San Francisco; right down the West Coast to Dana Point in Orange County South of L.A. On its route, it passes over the Golden Gate Bridge; goes through Santa Cruz and Monterey; right down the beautiful Big Sur Coastline; through Santa Barbara - holiday homes of the Mega-rich; meanders it's way along the many beaches of Los Angeles and then right out to the other side of L.A. at San Clemente. Officially, only the stretch from Oxnard, North of L.A., through to the southern end at Dana Point, is called "Pacific Highway 1" - but to me, and to thousands of other romantic, clifftop, winding coast route lovers, the whole, wonderful thing is Pacific Highway 1.........

I think the best part of *PH1* is the run down through the Big Sur area – crazy, winding cliff-edge roads with gleaming, azure sea shining up at you. However that was for after my big visit to Santa Cruz……..

Sunday - Santa Cruz

I was expecting SC to be really fun and interesting…….

"I thought Sant Cruz would be full of mad, quirky types - Hippies and Surfers and the like. People have been describing it like that to me - a really fun place full of characters.
Maybe it was because I was here on Sunday but I didn't get that impression at all."

As expected of a tourist, I first walked down to the famous Santa Cruz Boardwalk. Having read about its long history and obviously heard if its fame, I expected it to be a bit bigger.

"Basically the board walk is a very compact funfair on the edge of the beach. I rode the famous Santa Cruz Big Dipper - this was surprisingly good, made all the more frightening by the fact that it is very old and made of wood - looks a bit like a mining cart track when you are on it - like in Indianna Jones - but I don't think it is deliberate!"

Can you remember the route Indiana and his mates took out of the Temple of Doom?
(Yes I know my literary references are sorely lacking in substance). The Big Dipper was just like that...... except maybe not as safe. "How old is this timber structure?" I kept asking myself (I am a Civil Engineer as a day-job) and "Are the wheels supposed to leave the ground on the corners?". However, what was really frightening was the fact that you were sure your head was going to crack off the heavy, timber cross-members at the bottom of each dip. Classic American fun. I also went on a brand new rollercoaster too - this was rubbish in comparison. Multi-G thrills are nothing compared to age-inspired terror.

Being a little underwhelmed, I went for a walk around the beach looking for some action. However, being a Sunday, there were none of the "Spring Break!" crew around, just some male, beach-volleyball players which I strongly feel shouldn't be allowed.....

"Later, I took a walk back through the downtown area and back towards the hotel but yes, as usual, I took a wrong turn and ended up taking an unintentional detour of about 2 miles. Was a bit worried at first but most of the areas I walked through were quite well to do – in fact very nice, neat and prim. I did see one house in amongst all the other neat and tidy homes which was completely overgrown, had timber missing from the walls and had a peace and love, hippie, camper van outside - oh and they had their Christmas decorations up in the middle of summer"

That was the only piece of the Santa Cruz of my imagination I saw that day. Maybe I was just unlucky. As I said, the areas I walked through all seemed well-to-do. However, when I popped into a Petrol Station near to the Hotel once I finally found it, the guy behind the counter said:-

"Where did you just come from Man?".......

When I replied in my Scottish drawl – "Just roon there mate…", he said:-

"Man don't do that! People get shot and stabbed down there!"

It just goes to show how wrong you can be – no chain link fences, no rap music, no bouncy cars, just rows of nice wee houses. I could have been in Killearn (the nicest village North of Glasgow – cue the insults on Social Media).

I decided a chill out was in order. I would have another crack at Santa in the evening (as Mrs. Clause was apt to say…..).

Later I went back down-town to sample the nightlife. The following is how I described it the next morning – it is outrageous stereo-typing and probably utterly incorrect, both in fact and in the political sense, but I feel I should share the way the place struck me that night.

"I went to a couple of bars downtown. The locals seemed nice enough in these places, if a bit rowdy (a fair few fights and arguments going on), but there seemed to be a lot of strange Hispanic-looking guys hanging about. These guys were very quiet but in that way where they seem like, at any second, they are going explode into something utterly mental..... One sat next to me and asked a lot of slowly spoken and ever-more personal questions. I was about to quote the standard Scottish phrase of goodbye – "Beat it Wee Man!" when the barman came up and asked the guy how he thought he could sit in his bar drinking a carton of fruit juice that he brought in himself (fruit juice my arse!). The Trilby-hatted, moustachioed chap just looked at him for a few seconds and the bar man backed off. At this point I decided to exit the joint....."

No the bars were not comfortable and I'm from Glasgow….. I thought I would change tack – the food was supposed to be quite good.

"So I went and had something to eat in a restaurant for a change. Sat in the outside area of a really posh place……. and watched all the homeless pass by - not great when you're eating dinner."

That sounds terrible, doesn't it? "Bloody Homeless! No consideration for a chap having Suppah!". What I meant was that you feel a bit guilty eating a nice meal while watching less fortunate souls all around. However, on the other side of the coin, having paid a small fortune for a "posh" dinner, it wasn't so nice to have big, dodgy characters leaning over the trellis and glaring at you when you are trying to eat it…….

"When I had finished my dinner, I watched a big, ugly fight happen outside the bar I was just in and decided to walk back to the hotel where I went to bed early for a change. Out cold for nearly 9 hours - must have needed it."

"The way I see Santa Cruz is….."

(after my one day and night stay – hardly an in-depth study but one had to give one's opinion what?...)

" that it is a Seaside Resort. And like Seaside Resorts the world over it has its fair share of wierdo's hanging around. There are also a LOT of homeless. The positive side of that is, with Santa Cruz's reputation for Social Activism, there is a lot of help for homeless, especially those who are veterans. However, with Santa Cruz's Social Liberalism, maybe there is not a lot of control there either. There certainly didn't seem to be many Police around – cue the extended fights."

Don't listen to me – what do I know?.... Nuffink! That's what!

" Even the surf shops here seem to have been cashed-in on. You would expect them to be real surfers selling their quirky wares and skill-crafted boards but instead, the downtown area is full of mainstream shops pretending *to be surf shops such as O-Neil and Bill-a-bong."*

No, it's fair to say I wasn't impressed as I tapped out my grumpy blog the next morning. All-in-all, I think I was just in Santa-Cruz too briefly. I'm sure if I had stayed another day or two I would have found the quirky, surfer's paradise that I imagined. If I ever return I promise to take a bit more time and be a lot less grumpy!

SAVING GRACE! I happened to see the coolest guitar I have ever seen or will ever see again, in a grimy shop window. Made the whole thing worthwhile!

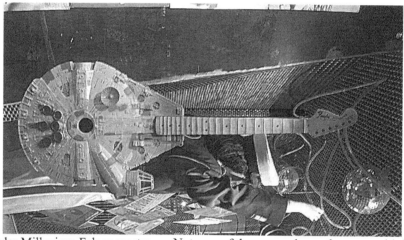

Fender Millenium-Falconocaster….. Not sure of the arm underneath comes with it or not…… would be handy.

Chapter 7 - Big Sur

A Biker's dream, a Hiker's dream, wonderfully scenic,
wildlife abundant......... and bloody Freezing!

Big Sur is not a place as-such. A practical description would be that it is
an area without settled boundaries. Having driven through it and walked
along some of its beautiful mountain tracks, I much prefer the romantic
description the Californians give it – that Big Sur is "more a State-of-
Mind than a place you can pinpoint on a map".

There are several different definitions of the area Big Sur covers but in
general, it seems to stretch from around Carmel in the North, to
somewhere near San Luis Obispo in the South – about 100 miles. It is
bound on the West by the coast and the wonderful "Pacific Highway 1";
and stretches Eastwards inland as far as either the foothills, or the
Western peaks, of the Santa Lucia Mountains, depending on who you
talk to. This is only 10 to 20 miles inland so Big Sur is small enough to
be as precious as it is made out to be.

The area is sparsely populated and has a spellbinding free-ness about it.
The coastal road is bike-heaven. The riding is challenging at times but
just enough for it to be fun without stopping you from enjoying the
wonderful cliff-tops, jagged outcroppings and sparkling, azure sea to
the West. You drop down into a natural valley between the cliffs and
find yourself concentrating on your line as you enter a nice, double-
hairpin bend with a sharp change in gradient. Having congratulated
yourself on the perfect combination of lean and power to negotiate this
like a Pro, you crest the rise and see a wonderful cliff-edge vista that
takes your breath away. I say again – bike heaven.....

Around 20 miles South of Carmel, the road takes a turn inland for a
spell taking you to Pfeiffer National Park where you can walk into the
foothills of the Santa Lucias. Here you can find the quiet free-ness for

which Big Sur is famed. It is still edged with a touch of danger though as you are warned about Mountain Lion attacks……..

The start of the run – Carmel by the Sea

"So I left Santa Cruz late morning - it was cloudy and cool which I was not happy about (come-on Mr President of the USA, do something about this - there must be something a few thousand troops could do) and headed down the freeway to Monterey where I could get back on "Pacific Highway 1". Was considering going to Monterey's famous Aquarium but instead passed by the whole town with 150 miles or more of windy coast road to negotiate."

I was disappointed to miss out on Monterey. Anyone who went to Crete in the hay-day of this original party-island, will understand the following: I imagined Monterey to be the "Hersonissos", to Santa Cruz's "Malia"…… (too obscure? *Someone* will get it). However, missing Monterey lead to me discovering a luverly wee seaside town with a difference. Now THIS was the "Hersonissos" to Santa-Cruz's "Malia".

*"Needing some fuel, I stopped at a town called **Carmel-by-the Sea**. This turned out to be a very posh, up-market seaside and surf resort with a difference. I had a browse in the town and found the shops to be full of such beautiful things that I bought a few prezzies to take home."*

As I rode in to Carmel I noted that this place was nice, in a rich and well maintained sort of way - lots of lovely big properties interspersed with trees and greenery. The first thing I found out about Carmel was that Clint Eastwood had been the Mayor (thank you to my wife for that nugget of golden info). However, Carmel has a bit more going for it than that. It likes to see itself as a dreamy, seaside destination for the cultured. The Carmel-California website states that "World-renowned Carmel-by-the-Sea has inspired artists, sparked romances, and attracted celebrities for decades". It also says that it is rated a "Top 10 destination in the US year after year" – quite a claim.

On looking into this further, I found that Carmel appears to be a town devoted to Culture and the Arts. In 1905 the Carmel Arts and Crafts Club was formed and as a result, after the San Francisco Earthquake of 1906 destroyed the Bay City; they were inundated with Artists, Writers, Painters and Patrons of the Arts. These fine types were offered cut-price plots in the town and began the swell of what has now become a massive Arts Community.

The town now has almost 100 Art Galleries within a square mile. It also has numerous tasting rooms where you can sample the Monterey Country Wines and get to know the "Vignerons". The town apparently has a history of Mayors who were Poets, Artists or Actors but the most impressive part of all to a heathen like me – it has a reputation for being Dog-friendly!

"After having a close encounter with some large, squirrel-like animals I had a walk on the beach. There was a seal just outside the surf barking away which I thought was amazing and took a load of video - however as usual I was to be proved wrong..... again....."

Yes I was practically mauled by a team of "critturs"… There was a massive, round bush in the middle of the beach and these little guys seemed to have a thriving community in there. Every now and then a team of them would come out and charm whoever was about to get some snacks then would run away back in with them….. Properly organised and professionally manipulative, these guys. This one furry-chap was kind of threatening so I gave up my wallet…..

Oi!..... Aye Yoo!.... Beef Jerky!.... Noo!

The seal out in the surf was a noisy mucker – barking away and rolling around. This added to the flavour of a very short and sweet visit to a new place. Eventually though, as always with us Scotsmen, either our bellies or our alcoholism takes control. As it was mid-morning the belly won…. just.

*"All of the shops in Carmel are full of fine art; antiques; beautiful, wispy, hand-made clothes and so on. The eating establishments seemed to be along the same lines. Due to this I was **forced** to eat something healthy for breakfast - avacado with olive oil on country toast. This was a new experience for me and I wanted to hate it, but it was rather good to be honest."*

Yes, this added another healthy option to my diet – so that makes two then…. I didn't have time to linger in Carmel but I have to say, it had a lovely, quiet, cultured way about it and would be worth a lot more exploring, especially for those who are Theatre Buffs or into the Arts. For a quick stop-off, even just a browse of the shops, it is definitely worth it. I bought some beautiful prezzies for, shall we say, some of the more senior, feminine members of the family…….

However, Big Sur awaited with teeth clenched….

Big Sur – a state of mind.

"Riding down this coast on a bike is 2-wheel heaven. Every time you come around one of the cliff top hairpins you are confronted with yet another fantastic vista of glittering blue sea, rocky outcroppings and dramatic cliffs. By this point, the clouds had gone to leave a beautiful azure sky and I stopped many times to take pictures to bore you all senseless with when I get back."

Yes, Big Sur made an immediate impression on me. It's hard to do justice to it without actually whisking someone down this road on the bike. A few pictures give at least an idea of the vibe…..

Check the sign out – sums this road up completely – Ace….

You get around 20 miles of these fantastic, coastal corners. Then, the road takes a turn inland for a spell. You start to see some beautiful forests with hills and mountains behind.

"Again, due to Lonely Planet, I stopped off at Pfeiffer Big Sur State Park and went on a bit of a hike up through the redwoods. This was only a few miles - if that - but was pretty steep and it was getting rather hot. One trail took me to an underwhelming waterfall (I had just seen the 617 foot Bradalveil Falls - come on) but the other took me to a view point way up above the valley which was pretty cool.

There were signs saying that hikers should make lots of noise due to the presence of Mountain Lions and also that children should be kept close as the Lions seemed especially attracted to them......."

I immediately began hatching a plan to bring my sons here…..

"When I got near the top, there were no other people and I began to wonder if I was meant to be going this far up. Suddenly I noticed that there was an animal trotting along the path in front of me. It was way bigger than a fox or a Marmot but didn't look like a Coyote. I couldn't get a good look at it – just glimpses. It was one of those film scenes when the heroine can't quite see the genteel chap in the reapers mask but we know he's there, don't we! Eventually it disappeared which just made me think it was toying with its new Glaswegian plaything.... Bring it on furrbaws!

"While I was sitting at the top, I chatted with a Japanese/American couple who appeared out of no-where. It turned out that the lassie had been in Vegas for exactly the same days as me last week - small world."

This was actually a really nice moment. We were looking right down a massive, tree-covered valley leading almost all the way back to the sea. We were all sat in a little green nook right at the top, just big enough for us all to fit in.... We sat there, just breathing it in like we were the only people for a hundred miles...... Sometimes though, the serene silence was broken......

"The bloke kept doing this high-pitched laugh at just about anything I said..... – alcohol-deprived paranoia was creeping into my brain and I had to exit stage-left....

Then, on the way back down (to make things more than a little surreal) in almost exactly the same place I had been toyed with by the animal of mystery, I took some video of a strange, furry creature up a tree which also appeared to be laughing in a high-pitched screech. Whether the creature was laughing at me or just at life in general I never quite established but ma heid began to burl...... A sharpish exit down to the reassuring safety of concrete and tar followed. Aaanndd, settle....."

There are many, many beautiful routes to trek in Pfeiffer National Park (not all populated by animals laughing at you) and plenty of camp sites.

There is also the Big Sur Lodge which has around 60 rooms. The park is named after John and Florence Pfeiffer who were early Pioneers of the area back in the early 1900's. Big Sur Lodge actually stands on the site of the Pfeiffer's original ranch where they used to house and feed any number of travellers visiting the area,….. for nothing……
However, after an unfortunate incident with an obnoxious, mule-beating traveller making Florence see red, they began to charge…… There's always one that flamin' ruins everything!……

A few miles further down the coast road is Julie Pfeiffer Burns State Park. This is named after another pioneering Pfeiffer of the time. There are good places to Scuba-dive here and also an 80 foot waterfall that drops off of a cliff down into the sea. I had to move on though.

"After an ice lolly with the last of my cash I headed back down the coast road - I still had over a hundred miles of this to do and it was already 5pm. The road took some very careful riding - really twisty and unpredictable. However, it was great fun and I was really enjoying it until I saw the cloud up ahead....."

Now here was something I didn't expect. As you work your way down the coast it gets COLD. Yes, it starts out reasonably warm in the sunshine, but as you go South there is often a sort of fog that comes out of nowhere and suddenly it is absolutely bloomin' Baltic! It really took me by surprise – suddenly it went from riding down the West Coast of California in the sunshine; to riding down the West Coast of Scotland in the dreich, damp, drizzley, dourness…..

"This thick, dark cloud that descends over the southern Big Sur area doesn't half keep the heat out. I already had my bike jacket on but had to stop and put a jumper on underneath. About 40 miles later I had to pull over and get my winter gloves and full face helmet on as I was FREEZING. However, this led to a really amazing experience."

"No!" I hear you say in best pantomime-watching croon…, "Not Another One!"…..

"I just happened to pull into this particular car park/vista point. It was completely random. In fact, I was going to pass it by as the daft driver who had been doing ma heid in for about 10 miles by going too slow, pulled into it as well. However, I was so cold I thought I would nip in and leave before he did.

While I was getting my gear on I heard a very deep bark from over near the sea. I saw a sign saying something about seals so went to check it out. I thought the seal earlier at Carmel was good.... I walked over to the fence, looked over onto the beach, and right there below were about 40 giant Elephant Seals! Further up were another two groups of about 40 each..... Incredible.

These things are HUGE. It is moulting season so they all lie up on the beach, lolling about and flipping sand, trying to shed their old layer of skin. They also spend a lot of time fighting and basically making a huge amount of horrible, burp-like noises."

The fighting these huge, blubbery beasts indulged in was pretty serious – a fair bit of blood was shed while I was there. The noises they make are so loud and disgusting they sort of remind me of "Doctor Who" Monsters. In amongst all the madness though were a couple: a huge male and small female who were lying serenely, their flippers touching like they were holding hands and letting all the madness go on around them. They were a couple completely at ease with each other and their surroundings.... I wondered if my wife and I ever looked like this to others...... Probably not (she's too slim and gorgeous to be likened to an Elephant Seal..... and too scary, let's not forget....).

"I reckon this was a once in a lifetime sight - all of these giant, endangered species right in front of you in their natural habitat. What a racket. Also there was a pelican in amongst them - brilliant."

Whit did yoo say wee man?!!!

The Happy Couple

I have since found out that this was not such an immaculately-timed piece of luck. The Seals started settling on this beach in the early nineteen-nineties and, as their numbers grew, the car park was built especially for the viewing thereof.... Thus – if you go down Pacific Highway 1 – just pull in to the Car Park a mile and a half past the Piedra Blancas lighthouse for an excellent show...... I wouldn't chance it around Valentines Day though - apparently, they are in full mating mode around then and that can't be a pretty site. It would be the sort of thing you would find going on in front of you as you leaned over the fence with your kids, having spent all day going on at them about how amazing it was going to be....... "Ahh it's not really as good as I imagined it would be Children. Let's go and have a look at that lovely, early model Ford in the Car Park!"

On a side note, seeing the Pelican reminded me of the time I had Pelican in a posh restaurant? It wasn't too bad but there was a huge bill.......

Mick Jagger-Lips

So, off to San Luiz Obispo then…..

Chapter 8 – San Luiz Obispo

How do they do that, is it a film set……?

"After the seals, I still had about 60 miles to go and I was REALLY cold. By the time I had passed Morro Bay it was dark and freezing. The last 12 miles to San Luiz Obispo were hard."

It really is quite incredible how cold it gets here. The fog just seems to suck all the heat out of everything – then you emerge out of it to the North of L.A. and it's hot again…. Freaky. The dark and fog drifting all around leant a real edge of mystery to San Luiz Obispo though. When I look back on this misty night, it seems as if I dreamt it – I was in and out the next morning but it made a real impression in mah stupit heid!

"San Luiz Obispo is a "College Town" which many people had told me was a really nice place. The guy on the desk at the hotel said that there were no trouble areas and that it was "completely safe to go anywhere". This was a phrase I had not heard on my trip and I was sceptical.

I headed into downtown about 10pm - a bit of a hike. Sure enough the place is really nice - tree lined roads, nice bars and restaurants, people cycling about, no "Bums" or "Bangers" and full of students. In fact, I must have been the oldest person in every bar I frequented – by about 10 years!

After a healthy meal of pizza (actually it really was healthy - loaded with vegetables and the base, instead of being dough with a tomato based sauce like normal, was actually JUST thinly sliced tomatoes.... Whoaahhh Dude.....)

I hit a couple of bars."

I know, it's just not like me but I thought – "what the hey…."

"Now I'm not an R and B man (except where it still stands for "Rhythm and Blues"). When you're a musician in Britain, R and B sometimes seems like pretty bland stuff. However, over here it makes sense. You go into a bar and the bass is pumping out and they are ALL dancing and having fun, ALL the time. R and B is at least easily memorised – everyone knows the words and this was actually a Karaoke - USA style. They were singing Jay Z-type numbers and all jumping about on the dance floor, all night…. I'll say one thing for Americans - when they go out they really make an effort to enjoy themselves – this is something I've noticed wherever I have been in the States (and Canada for that matter). The other thing I noticed tonight was that the geeky guys - the ones with the modern version of NHS glasses and their greasy hair all messed up - were getting all the female attention. It is cool to be a geek now. The rest of them were, well, let's just say there were a lot of baseball caps turned backwards with sunglasses. That didn't seem to be attracting the lassies at all…..

I stayed there for a good while until I started getting p'd off. Is it just me or are people losing the ability to assess personal space…. Combine this with the fact that a lot of Americans are huge and it can get a bit breathy and sweaty….

*Sick of getting buffeted about, I moved on and went across the street. This bar had live music. I got the feeling that tonight was for student bands to come and play a few numbers if they wanted to. There was a 4 piece up playing and no-one - absolutely NO-ONE - was listening to them. Well, knowing the amount of work it takes to get to a stage where you can go up and play as a full band in a public place, **I**, at least applauded them. They weren't three bad either. They had a lassie drummer (again in a geek outfit) who was really good and made maximum use of the 3-piece kit.*
When they went off (to no applause but mine…) I made a point of going over and telling them "well done" and how much I enjoyed it - which hopefully made their night.

It is a sad parody on modern music that this bar was almost empty at 1am whereas the dancey, karaoke across the road was still packed out and in full swing. Philistines!!!! A good stoning is required......."

Basically, that was it as I had to leave the next morning.... San Luiz Obispo – not particularly well-explored but clearly a friendly, safe and well-educated place. I am beginning to wonder though, how they keep it like this. How do they keep the tougher element out? In every town I have been to, there are supposed no-go areas, with shootings and stabbings apparently commonplace. Why not here? Is it a Film Set? Do they just not have any cheap housing and only allow students to rent homes? Do they monitor everyone who comes in and secretly gather up the "Bums" and cart them somewhere else? If so then this is rather Elitist to say the least, but I imagine there is a far simpler, less sinister reason... Food for thought though – would that be worth it to have a clean, law-abiding and settled town? Or is it just sinister...

"Anyway, the mighty L.A, tomorrow - dreading the freeway there as apparently, they all drove like loonies"

I didn't know the half of it.....

Chapter 9 – L.A. 1

The Freeway…………. Don't do it man!

"I am writing this at 6am after going to sleep at 2, purely because someone who shall remain nameless (but who's name is an anagram of nAdrew turCis) called on Skype and woke me up at 5am…."

This is the type of thing that is bound to happen when you fall asleep with your laptop beside you, watching an episode of "Sons of Anarchy". There is also the fact that "S.O.A." may not be an ideal thing to watch while on a solo Harley tour, especially after a good few "Bevvies"…….

From San Luiz Obispo to L.A. – Gathering Momentum

"It was a little warmer in the morning when I left – so it does get warm sometimes then….
Cruised down the freeway without a care in the world for a while then thought I would stop at Santa Maria for a bit if breakfast, some fuel and a walk around."

Now Santa Maria sounded like a really exotic, Hispanic-type place to me. Well it did turn out to be quite Hispanic I suppose, but riding through it, I didn't see much that was exotic. The problem with the American Grid System of Town Planning is that it can make places seem a little boring. Santa Maria is flat as a pancake and has the usual Boulevard running from one end to the other. Riding down this gave views of generic shops, motels and the odd trailer park and the other end led back out into the farmland. The surrounding streets were all pretty much at 90 degrees to each other and regular as clockwork.

To be honest, this was my problem rather than Santa Maria's. I had conjured up images of salsa dancers and gypsy weddings around the fire, purely from the name. At first glance though, Santa Maria turned out to be a regular, American town. I'm sure it is a great place to live and I hear is famous for its wine and special style of Barbeque (both of which appeal greatly to a Scotsman trying to be sophisticated) which might have swayed me to spend the night there if I had researched it properly. However, I instead stopped at a Mall at one end of the Boulevard (which turned out to be a pretty sterile and quiet place) where I had my third healthy meal in two days.

"Italian Salad for brunch..... You understand I had to be careful of toxic shock so I studiously balanced this out with a few meatballs in Marinara Sauce and a doughnut while glancing up hopefully at regular intervals in case some Flamenco Ladies suddenly sprinted in from the wings, dresses a-flowing...... No luck."

My ridiculous expectations dashed, I moved on.....

"Onto the freeway again. As I approached Santa Barbara it started to get a bit crazy. This is the L.A, drivers I thought – I can just about cope with this as long as it doesn't get any worse"

This turned out to be wishful thinking.... Things started to get a wee bit mental. Only a wee bit at a time though – the mental momentum was gathering.... However, first there was something more mundane to deal with.

"Hit a massive traffic jam and it was Hot Hot Hot. As it had been reasonably cool when I left, I hadn't bothered setting up my drinking tube from the rucksack and had my full jacket and Kevlar Jeans on. Result? Meltdown..."

This just reinforces the need to be prepared on a bike tour – one day you're so cold you need a full face helmet and leathers; the next you are so hot you need vented gloves and a drinking tube. Be prepared folks.......

Now up to this point in the trip, I had hardly done any queue -jumping on the Harley at all. It is not the most manoeuvrable of machines – in fact it is downright determined to go in a straight line. Also, as mentioned in an earlier chapter, queue jumping appears to be illegal in some States. After half an hour of slipping the clutch in the unbearable heat I decided it was queue-jump or pass out – so off I went.

"I should have started doing this sooner – squeezed through the entire queue and whenever anyone drifted in and it got a bit tight I just revved the engine. The bike gives off such a mighty roar that peoples' first reaction is to instinctively move away from it. Brilliant – got through the entire thing in about 5 minutes and away – and no "Punk-Ass Cop" at the end either!"

So this was all good so far – "Mad Drivers? Nae Bodgers!" I thought. I was soon re-united with the fabulous Pacific Highway 1 at Las Cruces. This would take me along the coast, all the way to L.A. This is a pretty incredible run. It just meanders its way along the shore with miles and miles of beaches running as far as you can see. At one point, as I approached Santa Barbara, there was a stretch where the whole side of the road was just Winnebagos, parked-up nose to tail, for about 3 solid miles. Some of them were as big as an Artic-Lorry Trailer and with special, extra compartments that stick out the side to give even more room. I have to assume that every one of these vehicles was full of surfers, waiting for the tide to go back out, as there was hardly a soul to be seen anywhere.... Bizarre....

Soon though, even this road began to get a bit mental as I neared L.A.

"At one point I was hammering along, keeping ahead of all the lunatics behind me when I came around a corner and found a just-crashed car, right dead-centre in the middle of the carriageway. The occupants were

standing at the side of the road looking generally nonchalant about it instead of maybe trying to clear away some of the debris….
Running at a fair old pace, I snapped a look in the mirror, saw the cars behind coming mighty close and just weaved my way through the wreckage like Ghost Rider and roared off again. Self-preservation - that's the name of the game down here."

"At least it can't get worse than that" was running through mah heid…..
Aye-Right!

Now here's a thing. Directions in the States can sound very like directions in the UK….., but be completely different….. A coolly-bearded chap in a Gold-Panning shop back up in the mountains had given me directions to a bar "where all the bikers go" near Santa Barbara. The directions were – head past Santa Barbara on Pacific Highway 1; turn left onto "Kanan" then take a right onto "Mulholland" and it is on your left. Sounds simple doesn't it? Maybe a few hundred yards up one street, then a quick tootle along another (no doubt at a nice right-angle to the first) and there it would be…..

What I didn't know was that "Kanan Dume Road" as I found it to be called, started at Malibu (around 65 miles *beyond* Santa Barbara…) then ran for 7 miles right up into the mountains before there was any sign of "Mulholland Highway" which (don't be fooled by the name) was another long, windy mountain road – this country is crazy. I missed "Mulholland" and ended up another 15 miles or so into the mountains on the windiest part of the trip yet – even more so than Yosemite – 1st gear around blind hairpins, slipping the clutch all the while. It was hot and I had no water and was running low on fuel. I knew I was heading generally towards LA but every time I came down a mountainside, there at the bottom was another one to go up. Each tiny village had no Gas Station and I was really starting to worry as the fuel gauge on these things seems to take forever to go down to half full, then goes from half full to completely empty in about 20 miles.
This went on for about another hour and it got to the stage where I was freewheeling down each mountain-side to save fuel, in order to get up

the next one. Finally, I saw a few palm trees and huge, gleaming houses and, thank the Lord, a Gas Station. The bike was missing and about to conk out just as I rolled-in. Somewhat relieved, I downed a litre of powerade, a litre of water and a pack of Beef Jerky… Better….. But for crying out loud – is it just me or were those directions Pure Pish!!! Never trust any coolly-bearded guys in Gold Panning Shops…

On a serious note, this is why you need to try to stick to your route (or carry extra fuel and supplies on your back). I planned my route throughout this trip pretty carefully. If I had stayed on the Coast Road beyond Malibu and followed it all the way into LA, I would have eventually come to LAX Airport as it is just off the coast. This would have involved minimal, if any, freeway riding and be pure, dead simple. Now, due to my little detour, I was North-West of LA and had to take Freeway 170 then 101 into the City. In the paragraphs above I have tried to show how the LA driving that I had been warned about had been increasing in craziness the closer I got. Nothing could have prepared me for the next few hours……. ENSEN! ENGAGE GRUMPY DRIVE!…..

"This evening was a horrendous experience. I will never, NEVER try to ride a bike into LA again. The ordeal went on for hours and hours and to be honest, now that I am here, I feel lucky to have managed it unscathed."

Good start eh? And being appropriately over-dramatic as well!

"The freeway into LA was just horrendous. I had been warned that they drive a bit madly down here but nothing could have prepared me for this. I avoided the freeway as much as possible in the afternoon, but after a bit of a wild goose chase, I had to enter LA on Freeway 101. I assumed that there would be signs to the airport as there would have been with any other city in the world - my hotel for the next 2 nights was at the Airport. I was wrong."

It gets grumpier.

"The freeway here is beyond anything I have ever seen. They hammer up all lanes at 100 miles an hour, weaving in and out and firing across each other's paths. There is no slow lane. They drive like absolute numpties. I have never seen anything like it - even in Italy."

Anyone who has driven in Italy, especially North to South over the mountains, will know that this is quite a claim…..

"I was just trying to hold my nerve long enough until I hit the airport, however, this ridiculous city has seen fit to only put up signs with street names on them. There were NO signs for the airport or for anything else. And the signs that they do have, come too late - you just cannot then change lanes in time as people are shooting up either side of you all the time – Oh for a fast, nippy sports-bike!. There are freeways criss-crossing all over the place and sometimes the centre lane suddenly turns into an exit lane which whisks you up over the top of others with very little warning. I kept being shunted onto different on-off ramps all the time. The Harley is not a zippy bike to say the least – last second changes in direction are not easy…
When it came to the 2nd last junction I got off and stopped in a street. I was just on the edge of downtown and had absolutely no idea where to go.
I got my map out but was VERY conscious that I would look like a tourist and I had no idea where I was. I asked 2 huge black fellers and they calmly explained what to do (which I think looking back was correct) but I just couldn't do it. I got onto the first freeway ok but then it came to an end before the one they told me to take and I ended up heading south towards long beach and had to get off again.

Where to stop?
*What kind of ridiculous state is a City in when you are worried about leaving the freeway **anywhere** in case you end up in an area where you will get killed. If you believe the Gangsta-Hype, this place is full of them - Compton. South Central, Inglewood….."*

This is actually a serious point though made in a grumpy fashion…. I wonder if American Cities are really as dangerous as they are made out to be. There are dangerous places in Glasgow but you wouldn't be in jeopardy just walking through them – at least not in the day time. If these areas are truly that dangerous then this country has a serious problem….

"Eventually I turned off of this, latest freeway and thankfully saw some blue, police lights ahead. I pulled in and, after he had hassled me for a bit (just because he felt like it – his sole occupation at the time was to be parked behind an injured cat so no-one would hit it on a massively wide, completely dead road through an Industrial Estate at night….) he gave me directions - another 2 freeways then up some boulevard going north.
I got on the correct freeways - the 2nd by the skin of my teeth - and after about 20 minutes finally saw a sign for LAX. Managing to leave at the right junction for once, I felt great relief when a plane flew over my head less than 100 feet above. This was a good 2 hours after my initial approach to LA and every bit fraught!"

"Aahhh, the end of the rant" I hear you thinking….. "Blessed relief…."

.

Well think again…. "Grrrumpy-Drive is Overloaded Captannnn… She's Gonnae BLOW!"

"This wasn't the end of it. The road that this led on to was massive, and lunatic. I thought the Sheraton LAX Airport would be easy to find - not at all. It was dark and I was knackered. LAX is quite near Inglewood and it would only take a couple of wrong turns to be in trouble. I eventually got some directions by going into the YMCA of all places. Even then I couldn't find the right road and had to take a few goes at it, really only relying on my sense of direction.

Finally I saw the place - this was 9.30pm. Got gear in and bike parked up - 19 flamin' dollars for parking."

So, I had made it. Stick to your route folks – turning off on the Kanan-Mulholland goose chase had caused hours of hassle - it was not fun…. However, I would also say that the Sheraton LAX Hotel is not the place to stay if you are spending a few days in L.A.. I had a couple of nights left and wanted to head straight out (we Scotsmen can't let our blood-alcohol levels drop too far - it's a medical thing related to the lack of sunshine) but this wasn't to be……

I continued…

"Now I am totally depressed……"

Ha Ha….Wheeeeee!!!

"This hotel is one of those huge, soul-less Airport Places. The area around about is predominately huge hotels with the odd rent-a-car thrown in. I asked the Receptionist where would be a good place to go. He leant over and told me in a conspiratorial fashion, "I can't tell you, you will need to ask the Concierge". The Concierge turned out to be a man of Eastern persuasion who was surly, abrupt and, in fact, downright rude which really stands out in a country where most people are usually super-nice to you.

He said that the only places to go were Hollywood Boulevard or Santa Monica Beach but they would be $45 dollars in a taxi each way. I asked him if there was a shop nearby and he pretty much shouted the following, well thought-out answer - "No!!!!". He nearly got a slap for that I can tell you….

Feeling a bit like Magnum P.I., I sidled over to his mate while he wasn't looking who eventually spilled that there was a convenience store around the corner which I went to and got some beer at least. I took this to my room as I just couldn't bear to sit down there and watch everyone coming and going to the airport with their luggage. The room was just as bad – no window looking out, just a window looking on to the corridor with everyone coming and going with their suitcases."

There is seriously nothing worse, on your last couple of days of a trip, sitting watching people going home. Moral of the story? Don't stay in an Airport Hotel!

A little later I asked another Employee where I could go for a drink but he simply said "It is not safe." I was getting a very bad impression of L.A. Was the entire City unsafe? What would normal people do at this time of night – just stay in their homes? It just couldn't be that bad….. I went to bed late, fed up and miserable.

"That can't be the end!" I hear you thinking…. "Even he's not *that* grumpy!" Well you're right. L.A. went a long way to redeeming itself the next day and all of this could have been avoided if I had booked a hotel in a nicer place – take this on board folks if you're travelling here!

Chapter 10. - L.A. 2 – Santa Monica

Venice Beach – just a big version of the beach at Ayr,
Scotland.... or the most wonderful mixture of fabulous
lunatics ever?

I woke up in the morning to find that my wife, still looking after me
from 5000 miles away, had sent me a link to a really useful bus website.
A bit of research showed me how to get to Santa Monica from LAX and
I headed out to the LAX Bus Station. Here I met an interesting
character who is the epitome of American free enterprise….

*"There was no information desk at the nearby Bus Depot. I was a bit
lost but then a HUGELY fat feller called me over and started telling me
all the different bus routes I could take, where to change and what to
do. All of this was gospel as far as I can see now. However, before I left
he asked me for "about 6 bucks to get some food". I actually gave him
6 but he said "wait a minute bro! Is dat all the change you gat? Cus
you'll need it for da bus, man."*

*He actually gave me my money back but said that if I just paid one way
it would only cost a dollar. So I gave him exactly half back which he
protested about, saying that I could give him all except the buck and he
was just looking out for me….. I didn't cave in and we parted on good
terms. When he didn't get on the bus and sidled over to some other lost-
looking souls, I realised that this is what he does for a living – gives
tourists advice on all the bus routes, tells them a saving, then asks for
money – pretty enterprising really."*

The reason this is so enterprising is that it isn't really a scam. I've seen
similar things going on at other busy transport hubs that *are* scams. For
example, at Shiphol Airport, Amsterdam; I eventually sussed that the
guys who come up to you at the train ticket machines, give you advice
on a saving to make, then ask for the change; are actually at it! The

saving you make is by you buying an incorrect type of ticket and, having given them the change from the saving, you end up having to buy another ticket…..

This guy on the other hand, was reading up on all the routes so he knew them inside out, giving good advice and asking for a reward for this useful service. I wish I had asked this guy's name – maybe someone reading this will know of him….

The Bus to Santa Monica took far longer than it should. This was largely due to the fact that every few stops, all of us standing had to get off to let a "wheelchair" on. "Nothing wrong with that" you are thinking and of course, you are right. The "Wheelchairs" in question though, were mostly these electric mobility scooters that you tend to see zooming around Supermarkets these days. However, after a while I began to realise that the (mainly) ladies in these carts were not old, were not disabled or mentally challenged,…… they were just hugely fat!

Yes I know I am on dangerous, DANGEROUS ground right now. I do realise that being obese is not necessarily a person's fault and that obesity is actually a form of physical disablement and hey, extracurvyladies.com is well-bookmarked on my PC. It's just that at that moment, the huge *amount* of people I had noticed in the States that were dangerously obese, finally hit home. After having that huge McDonalds in Vegas, I was put in mind of Americans in Britain, complaining about our rather frugal portions (refer to Fawlty Towers, episode 3 – "Waldorf Salad" if you want to be scientific in your research like I have….). I wondered now though, if this is actually something we do *right* in Britain….

"The bus sat for ages as one, huge woman took several goes at driving on. I had a chuckle when she couldn't quite manoeuvre her chariot around the bend so she jumped off it before anyone could help her, crouched down and LIFTED the whole thing (which must have weighed a good 40 kilograms) off the ground and chucked it around the corner. She then got back on it and proceeded to clip as many exposed ankle-bones as she could on her way down the aisle.

I didn't chuckle quite so much when we had to all wait for the whole process to be done in reverse when she got back off the bus,..... about 100 yards down the road!!!"

I eventually got to Santa Monica and went down to the beach. I walked along the promenade at Ayr in Scotland, then out onto Blackpool Pier..... Well, that's what it would have seemed like if it hadn't been 100 degrees and have the odd palm tree about. I was expecting roller-skating bikini-clad women and muscle-parks......... and Frisbee-dog competitions......... and bikini volleyball......... and roller-skating, bikini volleyball and......

Well-disappointed.... I decided to go for a run down the beach walkway and things definitely began to improve.... There were bikes and carts of all manner with families on them heading along the surfaced track which meanders through the sand. There were at last a couple of roller skating, top-heavy luvvlies, and it was getting hotter. Then...... I hit Venice Beach.

Venice Beach is about the coolest and quirkiest Beach in LA. This is where you see the bodybuilders working out on the edge of the beach, people getting strange piercings and tattoos and all manner of stalls, entertainers and shops – this was more like it. I spent several hours walking around and bought some really quite beautiful things (mostly for my really quite beautiful wife) many of which you could see being made right in front of you.

"People had come up with all manner of ways to try to make money – from the roller blading rasta playing Jimi Hendrix guitar as he went – to the man with the sign intimating that he required some money to correct the problem of an oversized Gentleman's Member..."

Mind you, I did have to tell the stoned, surfer dude holding that sign up that he had it upside down…. He said "Uhh huh, yeah duuuddde, ha ha ha, ah huhh….. Oh Right!"

"There were a lot of Ganja guys around and loads of surfer dudes on skateboards. There were fitness freaks of all manner and beachside gyms like playparks with gymnastic rings and tightropes and all sorts of circus-like equipment. There were even bikes that were actually a step machine – which powered the bike – weird."

I actually met this dude in Vegas, then again at Venice Beach. Talented Guy....

"Muscle Beach". They asked me to go in but I didn't want to show them up-like...

"Uhhh – like, YEAH-dude!" – Nice Bloke

B....E....A....Utiful....

"Had a couple of beers and some fine American Fayre and went down to the water. The waves were massive. Went in swimming until I swallowed about a litre of seawater then saw what I was sure was a stingray and retreated. Had a happy lie in the sun then went in again. This time I saw what must have been a jellyfish and retreated again!"

What a Wooss…. Us Scotsmen are not used to swimming in the sea "wi thi animawls"…. Due to our temperate climate, it tends to have the effect of reducing one's scrotum to a tough, brain-looking surface the size of an unshelled peanut. It is worth noting though that this fear of anything living didn't stop me from attempting several Daniel-Craig-shots of myself walking out of the water…. I think you can guess what happened to them…… DELETE!

"It was now about 7pm and I had had the forethought to bring a pair of jeans for eveningwear. After getting dried off and changed, I walked back into Santa Monica. What had looked like any other part of L.A. during the day, transformed in the evening. 3rd Street turned out to be a huge, pedestrianised area, a bit like Sauchihall st. in Glasgow. It was mega safe with children and families everywhere. A brief stop in an Adidas shop to buy a cheap t-shirt as mine was "mingin", and I went into a Marguerite bar which was showing sports."

Now here was a happy error made on my part. We are ridiculously precise in our measures of alcohol in Britain – NEVER do we see a bar man pourin' sippin-whisky free-hand like in the States. Everything has to be poured to exact measures using standardised, industry-wide measuring containers…. So boring.

"I decided to have a marguerite as I had drunk nothing but beer since arriving. I expected this to be a small, precise cocktail like in Britain. It was $9 but the guy said if I was staying for a while I should get the 3-for-2 deal.
"3-for-2?" – I'm Scottish and would have taken this even if I didn't want them – It's SAVING MONEY!….. Now it turned out these marguerites were double shot – meaning they have two shots of tequila and 2 shots of triple sec in each one (and American shots are BIG). The unusual part about this is that he didn't give me 3 glasses of Marguerites, oh no…. He returned with one, MASSIVE marguerite glass, full to the brim……. I estimated it probably held about a pint and a half….. at least!
It took me two whole hours to finish it……..Happy Days…..

I had asked a tough-looking Cop earlier in the day if it would be safe to get the bus all the way back to LAX at about 11pm. He said "definitely", which surprised me…. I went to find the bus stop (with an early flight in the morning) but was distracted by live music coming from a "British Pub" which I would normally avoid like the plague. As I wandered inside, I found a revelation….

The Beatles……..

Well,….., the "*Mexican* Beatles"….

These guys had the classic "Beatles" suits on, had vintage "Beatles" guitars, even had the original "Beatles" HAIRCUTS,……. but they were deeply tanned, leathery-skinned Mexicans. They were playing all the classic "Beatles" songs and had them down to a tee and were even bobbing their heads sideways in that bleedin' Paul McCartney way that drives me insane…..

"The best bit about it though, they had even practised the "Beatles" accents! Imagine a classically Mexican looking Gent in a wig, sidling across the stage and opening up with a low, drawling Liverpool accent:-

- The guitarist to the drummer – "what do you want tuh hear nowww?"
- The drummer (imagine Ringo Star's slow, low, Liverpool accent) – "oi wunt to hear the woon abowt the Octupoosss".

Absolutely superb! I told them this when they had a break then had a few more beers and some strange red stuff during their second stint….."

So that was being straight for the early flight buggered then…..
Eventually I left with a happy "heid" and got on the bus back to LAX. And do you know what – it *was* fine…..

I had had a great day and night – confidence in L.A. somewhat restored......... This was the final night of the trip of a lifetime. A few hours of alcohol-sweetened slumber and it was finally time to go home.

* * * * *

Home Time

"Well, here I am having a beer in the airport bar. Negotiated the LA roads fairly well today in order to: find a sports shop for a present I have been trying to get for the wee fellas since I got here; find a diner to have Egg, Bacon and Avacado Burrito with "Grits" – loverly; and finally to off-hire the beast at Eagle Rider L.A. All went smoothly and the trip is finally over.

As a footnote I would like everyone to know just how much I have enjoyed this trip – it has been everything I had hoped for and more. Thank you to everyone who gave me advice but most of all thank you to Lorraine, my wonderful wife who has been nothing but supportive about it since it was first mentioned.
Thanks Babe."

Well that was it. Memories of a fabulous place, well-made.

The final word?

"Whoa Duuuude…., **I'm** Scaddish!!!"

"AYE RIGHT!"